BEN JONSON

Ben Jonson (1572–1637) was a poet and dramatist. He wrote many comedies, including *Volpone* and *The Alchemist* and devised a great number of court masques. In 1616 he was made Poet Laureate; his poetic works included satires, elegies, songs in masques and plays, epistles and epigrams.

Thom Gunn was born in 1929 and educated at Cambridge University. He had his first collection of poems, *Fighting Terms*, published while still an undergraduate. He moved to North California in 1954 and taught in American universities until his death in 2004. His last collection was *Boss Cupid* (2000).

BEN JONSON

Poems selected by THOM GUNN

faber and faber

First published in 1974
by Penguin Books Ltd

This edition first published in 2005
by Faber and Faber Limited
3 Queen Square London WC1N 3AU

Photoset by RefineCatch Limited, Bungay, Suffolk
Printed in England by Bookmarque Ltd, Croydon

A CIP record for this book
is available from the British Library

ISBN 0–571–22679–5

10 9 8 7 6 5 4 3 2 1

Contents

THE FORREST

Introduction

1

There are many Ben Jonsons to be found in this selection, and each of them is a considerable poet. The poems here range from the vernacular patter of the songs by Father Christmas or the Gypsy to the formality of the 'Hymn to Diana', from the most savage epigrams to the tenderness of the epigraphs or small elegies on dead children, from Petrarchan conceits to the severity of 'Though beauty be the mark of praise'. I haveto stop, or I would go on for another page pairing the extremes between which he moves so easily. All I can do here is to comment on a few of his poems and try to describe the kind of pattern they create for me when they are put side by side.

His poetry (as apart from his plays) has always been surprisingly neglected, considering its variety, and surely one reason for the neglect in the last century and a half is that so much of it can be damned as 'occasional'. That is, much of it is elicited by external events, or is intended to compliment some noble, or is written to commend another person's book. And nowadays we tend to use the phrase 'occasional poetry' to indicate trivial or insincere writing.

Yet in fact all poetry is occasional: whether the occasion is an external event like a birthday or a declaration of war, whether it is an occasion of the imagination, or whether it is in some sort of combination of the two. (After all, the external may lead to the internal occasions.) The occasion in all cases – literal or imaginary – is the starting point, only, of a poem, but it should be a starting point to which the poet must in some sense stay true. The truer he is to it, the closer he sticks to what for him is its authenticity, the more he will be able to draw from it in the adventures that it produces, adventures that consist of the experience of writing.

I would like first to point to one of Jonson's poems most clearly occasioned by an external event, the 'Epitaph on Master Vincent Corbet'. It is probably not one of the poems that sticks out on a first reading of Jonson's poetry, it is modest and at first sight rather conventional. The beginning is indeed formulary, though there is a tranquil sweetness of tone that accords well with the sweetness of nature in the man lamented. The emotion, perhaps, is more of admiration and respect than of love, admiration and respect for a life that was 'all order, and Disposure'. Jonson, like so many of his contemporaries, looked up to the moral chastity of someone who *knew* what was right to do (and did it) rather than having to learn it from experience. ('Not to know vice at all, and keepe true state,/Is vertue, and not Fate,' he says in another poem.) 'Disposure': his admiration is also for the willed, conscious, rational *arrangement* of a life. Arrangement as in a garden (the nurseries of the mind):

> His Mind as pure, and neatly kept,
>   As were his Nourceries; and swept
> So of uncleannesse, or offence,
>   That never came ill odour thence:
>   And adde his Actions unto these,
>   They were as specious as his Trees.

The poem, though still lucidly written, concentrates here to a statement of some weight. For the arrangement that he admires is not one of counters, of fixed things, but of living qualities like plants in that they grow, need tending, encouragement, pruning, and have a past and a future of change. This gardener is the opposite to Candide, for his garden involves him in the essentials of life, is a type of experience and not a withdrawal from it, and may result in actions that are as 'specious' (splendid) as trees.

At this point in the poem there is a return from the figure of the garden to plain description, but description that shades into rather complex interpretation of its subject:

'Tis true, he could not reprehend;
His very Manners taught t'amend,
   They were so even, grave, and holy;
   No stubbornnesse so stiffe, nor folly
To licence ever was so light,
As twice to trespasse in his sight,
   His lookes would so correct it, when
   It chid the vice, yet not the Men.

That the last line is translated from Martial is perhaps a fact of larger importance for Jonson than it is for me. Whatever its source (and 'sources' are sometimes a bit like 'occasions') it emerges as a kind of discovery, the product of an exploration performed with a quietness and pertinacity suitable to its subject matter. After this passage the poem, it seems to me, returns to formula once more, but the formula is meant seriously, you could say it is being re-experienced – for if the last few lines afford no surprises, they are certainly not slipshod.

From this I'd like to turn to two far more ambitious poems, 'To Penshurst' and 'To Sir Robert Wroth'. These also seem to be 'occasional' in the conventional sense, in that they were written for specific people or families (in fact it looks as though they started as thank-you letters). They also are direct and plain in style; what figurative language they contain is far from startling. Yet for all the plainness of statement, both poems are full of small vivid touches that contribute a certain richness of detail, as when Jonson refers to 'some cool, *courteous* shade' or tells of hearing 'the loud stag *speake*'. Such detail suggests a kind of bounteousness to the noble estates he is describing. There is besides some pleasant classicizing in both, and some versions incorporated from Juvenal and Martial. In both poems, also, the verse movement has a variety within firmness that conducts the reader with great ease through the descriptive passages, giving such description the liveliness of comment.

About line 35 of the first poem, we realize that Penshurst is a kind of English Eden. Moreover, it is not based on guilt; here again is the admiration of chastity:

And though thy walls be of the countrey stone,
    They'are rear'd with no mans ruine, no mans grone.

The poem to Wroth goes into even more detail about what he has avoided, for he has never wanted

To blow up orphanes, widdowes, and their states;
    And thinke his power doth equall *Fates*.

Both poems are about the responsibilities of rank, the second concentrating on the moral responsibilities, the first on the social. The 'Sylvanes' and the translated bits from the classics are not mere decorations but are functional references to a moral and social tradition that Jonson sees continued from classical Rome to Jacobean England. In fact 'To Penshurst' tells us far more about the Renaissance views on rank than many histories or literary commentaries, as Jonson leads us from tenant to guest (the author himself) to the final anecdote about King James, which is told with such grace and ease that for the while it gives a certain dignity even to that cold and pompous man.

However, the coolness, the formality, the eschewing of any striking rhetorical techniques, the general sense of external occasion dominating the poem, the suspicion that Jonson is just trying to please the gentry, make a modern reader find such poems – initially anyway – almost distasteful. But I would suggest that the poem explores values that are genuinely Jonson's and genuinely those of his hosts, and that Jonson takes it as a matter of course that they are shared. It is difficult to put oneself into a time when admiration for rank was not snobbery, but we have to make the attempt, and if we can do so then we have a chance of understanding the ideas that Jonson is trying to embody in these poems. As to the lack of showiness in the style, it is clearly deliberate, and is an attempt to further

realize the Eden-like chastity of those values he is exploring so carefully. The Eden is not a garden of primitive luxuriance but a seventeenth-century garden 'all order, and Disposure', and the style is of a piece with it.

2

These two poems are successful attempts at English classicism, both in derivation and in invention. They have moreover the smoothness, control and urbanity that we associate with 'classical' writing. It is interesting that most of those who have succeeded best in writing so, i.e. within restraints both technical and passional, have been people most tempted toward personal anarchy. For them, there is some purpose in the close limits, and there is something to restrain.

Certainly there is also a wild anarchic vigour in Jonson, but unlike the kind of classicist I have just mentioned, he permitted himself to use it, and use it with wonderful success, as anybody who has seen the plays will recollect. And he was besides a master of rhetoric, in both the modern sense of rhetoric as showiness, and in the old and more neutral sense of rhetoric as that sum of devices necessary for persuading the reader.

Probably Jonson started his writing career by writing the additional scenes to Kyd's *Spanish Tragedy*, and he continued to try every 'style' he could, not feeling bound to stick with one and develop only within it. The critics had not yet begun encouraging writers to identify style with personality, and to move with stately idiosyncrasy through Early, Middle, and Late Periods that could be mistaken for nobody else's. Indeed, you may find an exuberant early-looking style and a sober late-looking style jostling each other in consecutive works by Jonson. 'Her Triumph' (from 'A Celebration of Charis') is probably a product of his middle age, for example, and it is as lush a poem as ever came out of Elizabethan or Jacobean England.

I have been in danger, so far, of overemphasizing the chaste and classical Jonson, and perhaps oversimplifying him. In the first of the Epigrams he exhorts the reader to 'understand' his book, which in the context of so much plain writing does not look difficult. But even with the Epigrams Jonson clearly means the process of understanding to be more than the business of merely comprehending the text. He is probably the best epigrammatist in English because he does not intend his statements to be light commendations or dismissals, but witticisms (however elegant) placed in the context of a society's whole experience. Understanding means taking them to heart, means – ultimately – *acting* on them.

But understanding becomes something far more difficult when we reach the baroque works like 'Eupheme', the 'Elegie on the Lady Jane Pawlet', and 'To the Immortall Memorie, and Friendship, of that Noble Paire, Sir Lucius Cary, and Sir H. Morison'. Quiller-Couch, evidently, found the opening of the latter so bizarre that he omitted the whole first half of the ode in his *Oxford Book of English Verse*. And it is difficult to us still, the difficulty being one of tone – even though we have the advantage of greater familiarity with the tonal ambiguities of Jonson's contemporaries than most late Victorians had. The anecdote about the infant of Saguntum was evidently considered appropriate to a serious poem, but it does not accord with our ideas of decorum. The difference between the seventeenth-century attitude and ours on this matter is rather similar to the difference in attitude toward puns. We find puns a form of forced and infantile humour, whereas they found them elegant and rather beautiful, like ingenious rhymes.

The difficulties of tone are less easy to abridge out of the 'Elegie on the Lady Jane Pawlet', which many a modern reader would accuse of ludicrous elaboration and insincerity. And I think to read it properly we have to make a far more rigorous effort to think like seventeenth-century people than we did with the 'Epitaph on Master Vincent Corbet' or 'Her Triumph'. Earlier I used the word baroque, and used it seriously: for example I

would ask the reader to think of paintings by Rubens (an almost exact contemporary of Jonson's), the large ladies of the court being judged by an elegantly dressed Paris, or being improbably wafted up to an apotheosis by angels as fleshy as they are – going to God's court with the same kind of pomp as they would to that of James I. What we must remember is that artifice is not necessarily the antithesis of sincerity.

Perhaps it is relevant here to quote from Christopher Isherwood's definition of High Camp, a term he invented. His character says: 'true High Camp always has an underlying seriousness. You can't camp about something you don't take seriously. You're not making fun of it; you're making fun out of it. You're expressing what's basically serious to you in terms of fun and artifice and elegance.' (*The World in the Evening*) And we can assume that the fun and artifice and elegance of the 'Elegie on the Lady Jane Pawlet' were considered by Jonson's contemporaries to be an essential part of what must have seemed a splendidly moving public compliment.

The poem begins as dramatically as anything by Donne. Jonson pretends ignorance of the ghost's identity but obeys her summons: 'You seeme a faire one!' Then he recognizes her, and his exclamations would be positively melodramatic if they were not so exquisitely modulated by the flexibility, the continuous life, of the verse movement. He is almost stone, he is in fact marble, it seems, and a marble breast is an appropriate enough place for Fame to inscribe the Lady Jane's epitaph ('it is a *large* faire table,' he says half-ruefully, he of the 'mountaine belly'). He is thus led to the apt inscription of her name and title in the poem. After a summary of her virtues, there follows the elaborate and beautiful description of her fatal illness and death. The elaboration is the beauty, the beauty the elaboration. She becomes a martyr, her soul addressing the doctors:

'Tis but a body which you can torment,
    And I, into the world, all Soule, was sent!

The scene takes on the ceremoniousness of a court masque as she makes her exemplary farewells,

> And, in her last act, taught the Standers-by,
>   With admiration, and applause to die!

It is total artifice, as in Rubens. Jonson then conducts her into a seventeenth-century heaven, and exhorts her parents:

> Goe now, her happy Parents, and be sad,
>   If you not understand, what Child you had.
> If you dare grudge at Heaven, and repent
>   T'have paid againe a blessing was but lent,
> And trusted so, as it deposited lay
>   At pleasure, to be call'd for, every day!

He continues and ends the poem with an evocation of the Christian's certainty of entering Heaven, and even here there is the same hyperbolic and 'staged' feel to the verse, from the detail of 'the Starres, that are the Jewels of the Night', to the exultant ease of movement in the last few lines, where the Christian

> Gets above Death, and Sinne,
> And, sure of Heaven, rides triumphing in.

To those who are repelled by the artifice as such, it might be worth pointing out that 'Her Triumph', which many generations have found so immediately satisfying, is hardly a *realistic* poem either. In it, Charis is drawn in a car by swans and doves, and the whole thing is full of hyperbolic compliment and stagey artifice. Where the 'Elegie' differs is that moral precepts and also wit come into it, and most of us are as ill-equipped to deal with such a combination as we are to appreciate Shakespeare's puns. Besides, it is another 'occasional' poem, though I would suggest that (unlike the 'Epitaph on Master Vincent Corbet') the occasion is largely one of Jonson's imagination.

The 'Elegie' and 'To Penshurst', in their different ways, both come from Jonson's public self, something that it is important to understand in Jonson as it is not in, say, Donne or Herbert. It was not a public self like Byron's or Robert Frost's – which were all personality, and personality, at that, drawn from the poems as if by a bad biographer. Certainly his personality, even his eccentricities, can be induced from the whole body of his poetry, but it can be done more because of the extent of the public exposure than because he made any deliberate display.

The public self appears in three roles in Jonson's poetry: as critic of literature and culture, as critic of society and morals, and as poet laureate (laureate either to the king, or, more loosely, to the nobility in general). The roles are not always distinct: you could say, for instance, that in 'To Penshurst' he combines all three. For his literary and cultural criticism is meant in the largest sense. He links the classicism of Sidney (as in the *Defence of Poesy* and the *Arcadia*) with the classicism of Pope (as in the *Epistles*): it is not merely a question of bringing Martial or Juvenal up to date, nor even of building up a national literature that can rival the classics, it is a matter of continuing the life and society that was behind the literature, evaluating, adapting, naturalizing it. So in finding the Roman virtues in a Kentish estate he was acting simultaneously as critic of literature and of society. And of course he was also acting as a kind of laureate to the Sidneys.

The public self, then, is probably what we first notice, as Jonson would have wanted, yet there is a fierce and intense private self within it, which accounts for many of the public self's virtues and which in quite a few poems has an independent life of its own. Some of the poems are openly personal, and in others the personal emotion enters, you feel, almost in spite of his intentions.

The least interesting of such poems are those of spleen and bitterness – I have not included in this selection the poems against Inigo Jones, or the completely nasty 'Answer to Alexander Gill'. But I have included the revealing 'Odes to Himselfe', which are somewhat similar to each other in many ways. The one he wrote on the failure of *The New Inne* is better in detail than in its scheme, which fails to convince me. The feeling in the poem is of total contempt and of badly disguised fear. The public are swine, and feed like swine; dramatists are posturers. The imagery is powerful – it is of filth, mould, rottenness, and stale sweat. Behind it is the revealed but unacknowledged fear that the public might just be right in having rejected his play, and that his mind might be following his bed-ridden body into helplessness. The remedy at the end, to 'sing/ The glories of my King', though elegantly written, lacks the power of the invective that comes before it.

The other 'Ode to Himselfe' is better in all ways. It is somewhat less abusive (the public here consists of small fish rather than of swine), and there is a greater dignity to the action proposed at the end – something we can believe in as a possible course for Jonson instead of the hyperbolic wishful thinking that came at the end of the other poem.

> And since our Daintie age,
>> Cannot indure reproofe,
> Make not thy selfe a Page,
> To that strumpet the Stage,
>> But sing high and aloofe,
> Safe from the wolves black jaw, and the dull Asses hoofe.

Two lines taken from his own *Poetaster*, and well worth taking.

Yet aloofness was not always easy to achieve, and we might question whether the classical aloofness of the statue or the star is such a permanently desirable position to take up. It is comparable to the chastity of him who is virtuous because he does not 'know vice at all'.

Certainly, as I have implied, such an aloofness or chastity was something Jonson admired because it was so difficult for him to achieve. He seems to have been torn between partial love and partial hatred for the world and himself. I suppose it is the tornness that he does so well, the fact that he is prepared to follow through his hard doubts and try to find a few things that he can depend on. He is the tough tormented man who wrote the following in *Timber*, his collection of aphorisms:

> What a deale of cold busines doth a man mis-spend the
> better part of his life in! in scattering complements,
> tendring visits, gathering and venting newes, following
> Feasts and Playes, making a little winter-love in a darke
> corner.

There is a wistfulness in the last phrase that is also found in 'My Picture Left in Scotland':

> I'm sure my language to her, was as sweet,
>> And every close did meet
>> In sentence, of as subtile feet
>>> As hath the youngest Hee,
>> That sits in shadow of *Apollo's* tree,

he says there, his writing being an example, incidentally, of the poetry he is describing: it is all ease and sweetness, like a madrigal with its varied line-lengths and its re-echoing rhymes. 'Oh but,' he exclaims, breaking the smoothness very simply by substituting a trochee (the first in the poem) for the expected iamb – and we get a clear-eyed look at himself, a fat man in middle age:

> Oh, but my conscious feares,
>> That flie my thoughts betweene,
>> Tell me that she hath seene
>> My hundred of gray haires,
>> Told seven and fortie years,
> Read so much wast, as she cannot imbrace

> My mountaine belly, and my rockie face,
>   And all these through her eyes, have stopt her eares.

It is a simple poem, in a sense, but I have never come across another like it. The aloofness of mountain and rock is forced on him by age, and he frankly would prefer a little winter-love. It is a poem of self-pity, and (in spite of all that I was taught at Cambridge) self-pity is something people feel often enough for it to be a subject worth writing about. It is unusual here in that it is without either an admixture of self-hatred or an impulse towards special pleading: it is dignified, completely unwhining, circumstantial, and even at one point slightly funny ('she cannot imbrace/My mountaine belly').

The personal feeling here is of far greater complexity than that of either of the 'Odes to Himselfe', and is also of greater authenticity in that it is nowhere *willed*. The whole question of willed feeling comes up again, however, in 'To Heaven' and 'On my First Sonne'; in fact it is, in different ways, the subject of both poems.

'To Heaven' looks at first glance as if it were all argument, but it is all feeling in the way the argument is conducted. It starts with careful, slow, qualified statement, the verse movement suggesting the effort after precision. It speeds up in the ninth line:

> As thou art all, so be thou all to mee,
>   First, midst, and last, converted one, and three;
> My faith, my hope, my love: and in this state,
>   My judge, my witnesse, and my advocate.

There is an effort to get things straight; and the repetition of the familiar trinities reassures him, so that for a couple of lines the emotion emerges pure and intense:

> Dwell, dwell here still: O, being every-where,
>   How can I doubt to finde thee ever, here?

The rest of the poem in its paraphrasable content seems to support the confidence of these lines, but in the actual writing is the result of somewhat mixed emotion. Having had the assurance of God's care, he still has to return to the difficulties of life: he rehearses them wearily even while protesting that it is not weariness that elicits his love of God. Again, it is like no other poem I can think of: the feeling in it is controlled, admitted, denied (it seems), and then perhaps converted, and is conveyed at least as much in terms of the verse movement as those of the words; the movement, by shifts of a caesura and shifts in degree of stress, keeping the statements in a greater sense of uncertainty than the words themselves would indicate. (The uncertainty could be demonstrated at greater length by contrasting the movement of these couplets with the movement of those, say, that conclude 'To Penshurst'.)

Willed feeling is even more essentially the subject of 'On my First Sonne', in which he is casting about for ways in which to cope with his loss. The first four lines are gentle, and it is almost as if he is taking refuge from despair in learning and 'conceit'. 'Farewell, thou child of my right hand,' he says, recalling the Hebrew sense of the name Benjamin. The conceit of the child as lent to its parents he uses also in the 'Elegie on the Lady Jane Pawlet', but here it is more bald, he is unable to play so amusingly with the familiar thought. And in line five the emotion breaks out (as it did in the middle of each of the last two poems I have described). 'O, could I loose (lose) all father, now.' He continues with questions that seem but are not rhetorical, questions he tries to still with another piece of ingenuity ('here doth lye/Ben. Jonson his best piece of poetrie'), which is at the same time fully felt, and ending with feeling that is neither easy nor ready-made, feeling about the dangers of feeling.

The emotions in these two poems are difficult, scrupulously created, and qualified: he cannot live with despair more than any man, but he also cannot pretend that willed equanimity is simple or constant. He was never more true to his occasions.

THOM GUNN

FROM PLAYS AND MASQUES

Echo's Song

Slow, slow, fresh fount, keepe time with my salt teares;
Yet slower, yet, ô faintly gentle springs:
List to the heavy part the musique beares,
  "Woe weepes out her division, when shee sings.
  Droupe hearbs, and flowres;
  Fall griefe in showres;
  "Our beauties are not ours:
          O, I could still
(Like melting snow upon some craggie hill,)
    drop, drop, drop, drop,
Since natures pride is, now, a wither'd daffodill.

(From *Cynthia's Revels*)

Hymn to Diana

Queene, and *Huntresse*, chaste, and faire,
Now the *Sunne* is laid to sleepe,
Seated, in thy silver chaire,
State in wonted manner keepe:
   HESPERUS intreats thy light,
   Goddesse, excellently bright.

Earth, let not thy envious shade
Dare it selfe to interpose;
CYNTHIAS shining orbe was made
Heaven to cleere, when day did close:
   Blesse us then with wished sight,
   Goddesse, excellently bright.

Lay thy bow of pearle apart,
And thy cristall-shining quiver;
Give unto the flying hart
Space to breathe, how short soever:
   Thou that mak'st a day of night,
   Goddesse, excellently bright.

(From *Cynthia's Revels*)

4

Song

Fooles, they are the onely nation
Worth mens envy, or admiration;
Free from care, or sorrow-taking,
Selves, and others merry-making:
All they speake, or doe, is sterling.
Your Foole, he is your great mans dearling,
And your ladies sport, and pleasure;
Tongue, and bable are his treasure.
Eene his face begetteth laughter,
And he speakes truth, free from slaughter;
Hee's the grace of every feast,
And, sometimes, the chiefest guest:
Hath his trencher, and his stoole,
When wit waites upon the foole.
   O, who would not bee
     Hee, hee, hee?

(From *Volpone*)

Song

Still to be neat, still to be drest,
As, you were going to a feast;
Still to be pou'dred, still perfum'd:
Lady, it is to be presum'd,
Though arts hid causes are not found,
All is not sweet, all is not sound.

Give me a looke, give me a face,
That makes simplicitie a grace;
Robes loosely flowing, haire as free:
Such sweet neglect more taketh me,
Then all th'adulteries of art.
They strike mine eyes, but not my heart.

(From *Epicoene*)

Karolin's Song

Though I am young, and cannot tell,
    Either what Death, or Love is well,
Yet I have heard, they both beare darts,
    And both doe ayme at humane hearts:
And then againe, I have beene told
    Love wounds with heat, as Death with cold;
So that I feare, they doe but bring
    Extreames to touch, and meane one thing.

As in a ruine, we it call
    One thing to be blowne up, or fall;
Or to our end, like way may have,
    By a flash of lightning, or a wave:
So Loves inflamed shaft, or brand,
    May kill as soone as Deaths cold hand;
Except Loves fires the vertue have
    To fright the frost out of the grave.

(From *The Sad Shepherd*)

Hymen's Speech

What more then usuall light
(Throughout the place extended)
    Makes JUNO's *fane* so bright!
Is there some greater *deitie* descended?

Or raigne, on earth, those *powers*
So rich, as with their beames
    Grace UNION more then our's;
And bound her *influence* in their happier streames?

'Tis so: this same is he,
The *king*, and *priest of peace*!
    And that his *Empresse*, she,
That sits so crowned with her owne increase!

O you, whose better blisses
Have proov'd the strict embrace
    Of UNION, with chast kisses,
And seene it flow so in your happie *race*;

That know, how well it binds
The fighting *seedes of things*,
    Winnes *natures, sexes, minds*,
And ev'rie discord in true musique brings:

Sit now propitious *Aides*,
To *Rites*, so duely priz'd;
    And view two noble *Maides*,
Of different sexe, to UNION sacrific'd.
        In honour of that blest *Estate*,
        Which all good *minds* should celebrate.

(From *Hymenaei*)

8

Vulcan's Speech

It is a *spheare*, I'have formed round, and even,
In due proportion to the *spheare* of heaven,
With all his *lines*, and *circles*; that compose
The perfect'st forme, and aptly doe disclose
The *heaven of marriage*: which I title it.
Within whose *Zodiack*, I have made to sit,
In order of the *signes*, twelve sacred powers,
That are praesiding at all *nuptiall* howers:

1. The first, in ARIES place, respecteth pride
   Of *youth*; and *beauty*; graces in the *bride*.
2. In TAURUS, he loves *strength*, and *manlinesse*;
   The vertues, which the *bridegroome* should professe.
3. In GEMINI, that noble power is showne,
   That *twins* their *hearts*; and doth, of two, make one.
4. In CANCER, he that bids the *wife* give way
   With backward yeelding, to her *husbands* sway.
5. In LEO, he that doth instill the *heate*
   Into the man: which, from the following seate,
6. Is tempred so, as he that lookes from thence
   Sees, yet, they keepe a VIRGIN *innocence*.
7. In LIBRA's roome, rules he that doth supply
   All happy beds with sweet aequality.
8. The SCORPIONS place he fills, that makes the *jarres*,
   And *stings* in wedlocke; little *strifes*, and *warres*:
9. Which he, in th' ARCHERS throne, doth soone remove
   By making, with his shafts, new wounds of *love*.
10. And those the *follower*, with more heate, inspires,
    As, in the GOATE, the *sun* renewes his fires.
11. In wet AQUARIUS stead, reignes he, that showres
    Fertilitie upon the *geniall* bowres.

12. Last, in the FISHES place, sits he, doth say;
     In married joyes, all should be dumbe, as they.
     And this hath VULCAN, for his VENUS, done,
     To grace the chaster triumph of her *sonne.*

(From *The Haddington Masque*)

Charms of the Witches

1

Dame, Dame, the watch is set:
Quickly come, we all are met.
From the lakes, and from the fennes,
From the rockes, and from the dennes,
From the woods, and from the caves,
From the Church-yards, from the graves,
From the dungeon, from the tree,
That they die on, here are wee.

Comes she not, yet?
Strike another heate.

2

The weather is fayre, the wind is good,
Up, Dame, o' your Horse of wood:
Or else, tuck up your gray frock,
And sadle your Goate, or your greene Cock,
And make his bridle a bottome of thrid,
To roule up how many miles you have rid.
   Quickly, come away:
   For we, all, stay.

   Not yet? Nay, then,
   Wee'll try her agen.

3

The Owle is abroad, the Bat, and the Toade,
   And so is the Cat-a-Mountaine;
The Ant, and the Mole sit both in a hole,
   And Frog peepes out o' the fountayne;
The Dogges, they do bay, and the Timbrells play,

The Spindle is now a turning;
The Moone it is red, and the starres are fled,
    And all the Skye is a burning:
The Ditch is made, and our nayles the spade,
With pictures full, of waxe, and of wooll;
Theyr livers I stick, with needles quick
There lacks but the blood, to make up the flood.
    Quickly, Dame, then; bring your part in,
    Spur, spur upon little Martin,
    Merely, merely, make him sayle,
    A worme in his mouth, and a thorne in's tayle,
    Fire above, and fire below,
    With a Whip, i' your hand, to make him goe.
    O, now, shee's come!
    Let all be dumbe.

(From *The Masque of Queenes*)

Satyr's Song

Now, my cunning lady; Moone,
Can you leave the side, so soone,
   Of the boy, you keepe so hid?
Mid-wife JUNO sure will say,
This is not the proper way
   Of your palenesse to be rid.
But, perhaps, it is your grace
To weare sicknesse i' your face,
   That there might be wagers laid,
   Still, by fooles, you are a maid.
Come, your changes overthrow
What your looke would carry so;
Moone, confesse then, what you are.
And be wise, and free to use
Pleasures, that you now doe loose;
   Let us *Satyres* have a share.
Though our forms be rough, & rude,
Yet our acts may be endew'd
   With more vertue: Every one
   Cannot be ENDYMION.

(From *Oberon*)

Song

What just excuse had aged *Time*,
  His wearie limbes now to have eas'd,
And sate him downe without his crime,
  While every thought was so much pleas'd!
For he so greedie to devoure
  His owne, and all that hee brings forth,
Is eating every piece of houre
  Some object of the rarest worth.
Yet this is rescued from his rage,
As not to die by time, or age.
  For beautie hath a living name,
  And will to heaven, from whence it came.

(From *Love Freed from Ignorance and Folly*)

Cyclope's Song

Soft, subtile fire, thou soule of art,
   Now doe thy part
On weaker Nature, that through age is lamed.
   Take but thy time, now she is old,
   And the Sunne her friend growne cold,
She will no more, in strife with thee be named.

Looke, but how few confesse her now,
   In cheeke or browe!
From every head, almost, how she is frighted!
   The very age abhorres her so,
   That it learnes to speake and goe
As if by art alone it could be righted.

(From *Mercurie Vindicated*)

Father Christmas' Song

Now their intent, is about to present
    with all the appurtenances
A right *Christmas*, as of old it was,
    to be gathered out of the Dances.

Which they doe bring, and afore the King,
    the Queene, and Prince, as it were now
Drawne here by Love; who, over and above,
    doth draw himselfe i' the geere too.

Hum drum, sauce for a Coney;
    no more of your Martiall musicke:
Even for the sake, o' the next new stake,
    for there I doe meane to use it.

And now to yee, who in place are to see,
    with Roll and Farthingale hooped:
I pray you know, though he want his bow,
    by the wings, that this is *Cupid*.

He might goe backe, for to cry what you lack,
    but that were not so wittie:
His Cap, and Coat, are enough to note
    that he is the Love o' the Cittie.

And he leades on, though he now be gon,
    for that was onely his-rule:
But now comes in, *Tom* of Bosomes Inne,
    and he presenteth *Mis-rule*.

Which you may know, by the very show,
    albeit you never aske it:
For there you may see what his Ensignes bee,
    the Rope, the Cheese, and the Basket.

This *Carol* plaies, and has beene in his dayes
    a chirping boy, and a kill-pot:
Kit Cobler it is, I'me a Father of his,
    and he dwells in the lane, cal'd Fil-pot.

But who is this? O, my daughter *Sis*
    Mince-pie, with her doe not dally
On paine o' your life: She's an honest Cooks wife,
    and comes out of Scalding-Alley.

Next in the trace, comes *Gambol* in place,
    and to make my tale the shorter:
My Sonne *Hercules*, tane, out of Distaffe-lane,
    but an active man, and a Porter.

Now *Post* and *Paire*, old Christmasses heire,
    doth make and a gingling Sally:
And wott you who, 'tis one of my two
    Sons, Cardmakers in Pur-alley.

Next in a trice, with his boxe and his Dice,
    Mac-pippin my Son, but younger,
Brings *Mumming* in; and the knave will win,
    for a' is a Costermonger.

But *New-years-gift*, of himselfe makes shift
    to tell you what his name is:
With Orenge on head, and his Gingerbread,
    Clem Waspe of Honey-lane 'tis.

This I you tell, is our jolly *Wassell*,
    and for Twelfe-night more meet too:
She workes by the Ell, and her name is *Nell*,
    and she dwells in Thred-needle-street too.

Then *Offering* he, with his Dish, and his Tree,
    that in every great house keepeth;
Is by my Sonne, young *Little-worth* done,
    and in Penny-rich-street he sleepeth.

Last, *Baby-cake*, that an end doth make
   of Christmas merrie, merrie vaine-a,
Is *Child Rowlan*, and a straight young man,
   though he come out of Crooked-lane-a.

There should have beene, and a dozen I wene,
   but I could finde but one more
Child of Christmas, and a *Logge* it was,
   when I them all had gone ore.

I prayed him, in a time so trim,
   that he would make one to praunce it:
And I my selfe, would have beene the twelfe,
   o, but *Log* was to heavie to dance it.

   (From *Christmas His Masque*)

18

Song for Comus

Roome, roome, make roome for the bouncing belly,
First father of Sauce, and deviser of gelly,
Prime master of arts, and the giver of wit,
That found out the excellent engine, the spit,
The plough, and the flaile, the mill, and the Hoppar,
The hutch, and the bowlter, the furnace, and coppar,
The Oven, the bavin, the mawkin, and peele,
The harth, and the range, the dog, and the wheele.
He, he first invented both hogshead and Tun,
The gimblet, and vice too; and taught 'em to run.
And since, with the funnel, an hyppocras bag
H'has made of himself, that now he cries swag.
Which showes, though the pleasure be but of fowre inches,
Yet he is a weesell, the gullet that pinches,
Of any delight: and not spares from the back
What-ever, to make of the belly a sack:
Haile, haile, plump Panch, O the founder of tast
For freash meates, or powlderd, or pickle, or past.
Devourer of broil'd, bak'd, rosted, or sod,
And emptier of cups, be they even, or odd.
All which have now made thee, so wide i' the waste
As scarce with no pudding thou art to be lac'd:
But eating and drinking, untill thou dost nod
Thou break'st all thy girdles, and break'st forth a god.

(From *Pleasure Reconcil'd to Vertue*)

Two Songs Sung by Daedalus
(to precede dances)

1

Come on, come on; and where you goe,
   So enter-weave the curious knot,
As ev'n th'observer scarce may know
   Which lines are Pleasures, and which not.
First, figure out the doubtfull way
   At which, a while all youth shold stay,
   Where she and Vertue did contend
   Which should have Hercules to frend.
Then, as all actions of mankind
   Are but a Laborinth, or maze,
   So let your Daunces be entwin'd,
   Yet not perplex men, unto gaze.
But measur'd, and so numerous too,
   As men may read each act you doo.
And when they see the Graces meet,
   Admire the wisdom of your feet.
For Dauncing is an exercise
   Not only shews the movers wit,
But maketh the beholder wise,
   As he hath powre to rise to it.

2

O more, and more; this was so well,
   As praise wants half his voice, to tell;
      Againe yourselves compose,
And now put all the aptness on
   Of figure, that proportion
      Or colour can disclose.
That if those silent arts were lost,
   Designe, and Picture: they might boast

From you a newer ground:
Instructed to the heightning sence
   Of dignitie, and reverence,
     In your true motions found:
Begin, begin; for looke, the faire
   Do longing listen, to what aire
     You forme your second touch,
That they may vent their murmuring hymnes
   Just to the tune you move your limbes,
     And wish their owne were such.
   Make haste, make haste, for this
     The Laborinth of Beautie is.

(From *Pleasure Reconcil'd to Vertue*)

Gypsy Song

From the famous Peake of Darby
And the Devills arse there hard by,
Where we yearly keepe our musters,
Thus th' Aegiptians throng in clusters.

Be not frighted with our fashion,
Though wee seeme a tatter'd nation;
Wee account our ragges our riches,
So our trickes exceed our stitches.

Give us Bacon, rindes of wallnutts,
Shelles of Cockles and of small-nuttes,
Ribandes, belles, and saffrond linnen,
All the world is ours to winne in.

Knacks we have that will delight you,
Slightes of hand that will invite you
To indure our tawney faces,
And not cause you cut your laces.

All your fortunes we can tell yee,
Be they for your backe or bellye,
In the moodes too, and the tenses,
That may fitt your fine five sences.

Drawe but then your gloves, we pray you,
And sit still, we will not fray you,
For, though wee be here at Burly,
Wee'd be lothe to make a hurly.

(From *The Gypsies Metamorphos'd*)

Two Gypsy Songs

1

The faery beame upon you,
The starres to glister on you,
   A Moone of light
   In the Noone of night,
Till the firedrake hath oregon you.

The wheele of fortune guide you,
The Boy with the bowe beside you
   Runne ay in the way
   Till the birde of day
And the luckier lott betide you.

2

To the old, longe life and treasure,
To the young, all healthe and pleasure,
   To the faire, theire face
   With eternall grace,
And the foule to be lov'd at leasure.

To the wittie, all cleare mirrors,
To the foolishe, their darke errors,
   To the lovinge sprite
   A secure delight,
To the jealous his owne false terrors.

(From *The Gypsies Metamorphos'd*)

Sea Song

PROTEUS

Come, noble *Nymphs*, and doe not hide
The joyes, for which you so provide:

SARON

If not to mingle with the men,
What doe you here? Go home agen.

PORTUNUS

   Your dressings doe confesse,
By what we see, so curious parts
Of *Pallas*, and *Arachnes* arts,
   That you could meane no lesse.

PROTEUS

Why doe you weare the Silkewormes toyles;
Or glory in the shellfish spoyles?
Or strive to shew the graines of ore
That you have gathered on the shore,
   Whereof to make a stocke
To graft the greener Emerald on,
Or any better-water'd stone?

SARON

   Or Ruby of the rocke?

PROTEUS

Why do you smell of Amber-gris,
Of which was formed *Neptunes* Neice,
The Queene of Love; unlesse you can,
Like Sea-borne *Venus*, love a man?

24

SARON

Try, put your selves unto't. .

CHORUS

Your lookes, your smiles, and thoughts that meete,
Ambrosian hands, and silver feete,
Doe promise you will do't.

(From *Neptunes Triumph*)

Song

ZEPHYRUS

Come forth, come forth, the gentle *Spring*,
And carry the glad newes, I bring,
   To Earth, our common mother:
It is decreed, by all the Gods,
The Heav'n, of Earth shall have no oddes,
   But one shall love another:

Their glories they shall mutuall make,
Earth looke on Heaven, for Heavens sake;
   Their honours shall bee even:
All æmulation cease, and jarres;
Jove will have Earth to have her starres,
   And lights, no lesse then Heaven.

SPRING

It is alreadie done, in flowers
As fresh, and new as are the howres,
   By warmth of yonder Sunne.
But will be multipli'd on us,
If from the breath of ZEPHYRUS
   Like favour we have wonne.

ZEPHYRUS

Give all to him: His is the dew,
The heate, the humor,

SPRING

              —All the true-
Beloved of the *Spring*!

ZEPHYRUS

The Sunne, the Wind, the Verdure!

SPRING

                —All,
That wisest Nature cause can call
  Of quick'ning any thing.

  (From *Chloridia*)

EPIGRAMMES

To the Reader

Pray thee, take care, that tak'st my booke in hand,
  To reade it well: that is, to understand.

To my Booke

It will be look'd for, booke, when some but see
    Thy title, *Epigrammes*, and nam'd of mee,
Thou should'st be bold, licentious, full of gall,
    Wormewood, and sulphure, sharpe, and tooth'd withall;
Become a petulant thing, hurle inke, and wit,
    As mad-men stones: not caring whom they hit.
Deceive their malice, who could wish it so.
    And by thy wiser temper, let men know
Thou are not covetous of least selfe-fame,
    Made from the hazard of anothers shame:
Much lesse with lewd, prophane, and beastly phrase,
    To catch the worlds loose laughter, or vaine gaze.
He that departs with his owne honesty
    For vulgar praise, doth it too dearely buy.

On some-thing, that walkes some-where

At court I met it, in clothes brave enough,
   To be a courtier; and lookes grave enough,
To seeme a statesman: as I neere it came,
   It made me a great face, I ask'd the name.
A lord, it cryed, buried in flesh, and blood,
   And such from whom let no man hope least good,
For I will doe none: and as little ill,
   For I will dare none. Good Lord, walke dead still.

To Doctor Empirick

When men a dangerous disease did scape,
   Of old, they gave a cock to AESCULAPE;
Let me give two: that doubly am got free,
   From my diseases danger, and from thee.

To William Camden

Camden, most reverend head, to whom I owe
   All that I am in arts, all that I know,
(How nothing's that?) to whom my countrey owes
   The great renowne, and name wherewith shee goes.
Then thee the age sees not that thing more grave,
   More high, more holy, that shee more would crave.
What name, what skill, what faith hast thou in things!
   What sight in searching the most antique springs!
What weight, and what authoritie in thy speech!
   Man scarse can make that doubt, but thou canst teach.
Pardon free truth, and let thy modestie,
   Which conquers all, be once over-come by thee.
Many of thine this better could, then I,
   But for their powers, accept my pietie.

On my first Daughter

Here lyes to each her parents ruth,
MARY, the daughter of their youth:
Yet, all heavens gifts, being heavens due,
It makes the father, lesse, to rue.
At sixe moneths end, shee parted hence
With safetie of her innocence;
Whose soule heavens Queene, (whose name shee beares)
In comfort of her mothers teares,
Hath plac'd amongst her virgin-traine:
Where, while that sever'd doth remaine,
This grave partakes the fleshly birth.
Which cover lightly, gentle earth.

To Sir Annual Tilter

Tilter, the most may'admire thee, though not I:
   And thou, right guiltlesse, may'st plead to it, why?
For thy late sharpe device. I say 'tis fit
   All braines, at times of triumph, should runne wit.
For then, our water-conduits doe runne wine;
   But that's put in, thou'lt say. Why, so is thine.

On Chev'rill the Lawyer

No cause, nor client fat, will CHEV'RILL leese,
   But as they come, on both sides he takes fees,
And pleaseth both. For while he melts his greace
   For this: that winnes, for whom he holds his peace.

On Margaret Ratcliffe

M arble, weepe, for thou dost cover
A dead beautie under-neath thee,
R ich, as nature could bequeath thee:
G rant then, no rude hand remove her.
A ll the gazers on the skies
R ead not in faire heavens storie,
E xpresser truth, or truer glorie,
T hen they might in her bright eyes.
R are, as wonder, was her wit;
A nd like *Nectar* ever flowing:
T ill time, strong by her bestowing,
C onquer'd hath both life and it.
L ife, whose griefe was out of fashion,
I n these times. Few so have ru'de
F ate, in a brother. To conclude,
F or wit, feature, and true passion,
E arth, thou hast not such another.

On Gypsee

Gypsee, new baud, is turn'd physitian,
   And get more gold, then all the colledge can:
Such her quaint practise is, so it allures,
   For what she gave, a whore; a baud, shee cures.

On my First Sonne

Farewell, thou child of my right hand, and joy;
   My sinne was too much hope of thee, lov'd boy,
Seven yeeres tho'wert lent to me, and I thee pay,
   Exacted by thy fate, on the just day.
O, could I loose all father, now. For why
   Will man lament the state he should envie?
To have so soone scap'd worlds, and fleshes rage,
   And, if no other miserie, yet age?
Rest in soft peace, and, ask'd, say here doth lye
   BEN. JONSON his best piece of *poetrie*.
For whose sake, hence-forth, all his vowes be such,
   As what he loves may never like too much.

To Play-wright

Play-wright me reades, and still my verses damnes,
    He sayes, I want the tongue of *Epigrammes*;
I have no salt: no bawdrie he doth meane.
    For wittie, in his language, is obscene.
PLAY-WRIGHT, I loath to have thy manners knowne
    In my chast booke: professe them in thine owne.

On Spies

Spies, you are lights in state, but of base stuffe,
Who, when you'have burnt your selves downe to the snuffe,
Stinke, and are throwne away. End faire enough.

To Fine Lady Would-bee

Fine MADAME WOULD-BE, wherefore should you feare,
    That love to make so well, a child to beare?
The world reputes you barren: but I know
    Your 'pothecarie, and his drug sayes no.
Is it the paine affrights? that's soone forgot.
    Or your complexions losse? you have a pot,
That can restore that. Will it hurt your feature?
    To make amends, yo'are thought a wholesome creature.
What should the cause be? Oh, you live at court:
    And there's both losse of time, and losse of sport
In a great belly. Write, then on thy wombe,
    Of the not borne, yet buried, here's the tombe.

On Lippe, the Teacher

I cannot thinke there's that antipathy
   'Twixt *puritanes*, and *players*, as some cry;
Though LIPPE, at PAULS, ranne from his text away,
   T'inveigh 'gainst playes: what did he then but play?

To Proule the Plagiary

Forbeare to tempt me, PROULE, I will not show
   A line unto thee, till the world it know;
Or that I'have by, two good sufficient men,
   To be the wealthy witnesse of my pen:
For all thou hear'st, thou swear'st thy selfe didst doo.
   Thy wit lives by it, PROULE, and belly too.
Which, if thou leave not soone (though I am loth)
   I must a libell make, and cosen both.

To Sir Henry Goodyere

GOODYERE, I'am glad, and gratefull to report,
  My selfe a witnesse of thy few dayes sport:
Where I both learn'd, why wise-men hawking follow,
  And why that bird was sacred to APOLLO,
Shee doth instruct men by her gallant flight,
  That they to knowledge so should toure upright,
And never stoupe, but to strike ignorance:
  Which if they misse, they yet should re-advance
To former height, and there in circle tarrie,
  Till they be sure to make the foole their quarrie.
Now, in whose pleasures I have this discerned,
  What would his serious actions me have learned?

To Lucy, Countesse of Bedford,
with Mr Donnes Satyres

LUCY, you brightnesse of our spheare, who are
    Life of the *Muses* day, their morning-starre!
If workes (not th'authors) their owne grace should looke,
    Whose poemes would not wish to be your booke?
But these, desir'd by you, the makers ends
    Crowne with their owne. Rare poemes aske rare friends.
Yet, *Satyres*, since the most of mankind bee
    Their un-avoided subject, fewest see:
For none ere tooke that pleasure in sinnes sense,
    But, when they heard it tax'd, tooke more offence.
They, then, that living where the matter is bred,
    Dare for these poemes, yet, both aske, and read,
And like them too; must needfully, though few,
    Be of the best: and 'mongst those, best are you.
LUCY, you brightnesse of our spheare, who are
    The *Muses* evening, as their morning-starre.

To John Donne

Who shall doubt, DONNE, where I a *Poet* bee,
   When I dare send my *Epigrammes* to thee?
That so alone canst judge, so'alone dost make:
   And, in thy censures, evenly, dost take
As free simplicitie, to dis-avow,
   As thou hast best authoritie, t'allow.
Reade all I send: and, if I find but one
   Mark'd by thy hand, and with the better stone,
My title's seal'd. Those that for claps doe write,
   Let pui'nees, porters, players praise delight,
And, till they burst, their backs, like asses load:
   A man should seeke great glorie, and not broad.

Inviting a friend to supper

To night, grave sir, both my poore house, and I
    Doe equally desire your companie:
Not that we thinke us worthy such a ghest,
    But that your worth will dignifie our feast,
With those that come; whose grace may make that seeme
    Something, which, else, could hope for no esteeme.
It is the faire acceptance, Sir, creates
    The entertaynment perfect: not the cates.
Yet shall you have, to rectifie your palate,
    An olive, capers, or some better sallade
Ushring the mutton; with a short-leg'd hen,
    If we can get her, full of egs, and then,
Limons, and wine for sauce: to these, a coney
    Is not to be despair'd of, for our money;
And, though fowle, now, be scarce, yet there are clarkes,
    The skie not falling, thinke we may have larkes.
Ile tell you of more, and lye, so you will come:
    Of partrich, pheasant, wood-cock, of which some
May yet be there; and godwit, if we can:
    Knat, raile, and ruffe too. How so ere, my man
Shall reade a piece of VIRGIL, TACITUS,
    LIVIE, or of some better booke to us,
Of which wee'll speake our minds, amidst our meate;
    And Ile professe no verses to repeate:
To this, if ought appeare, which I not know of,
    That will the pastrie, not my paper, show of.
Digestive cheese, and fruit there sure will bee;
    But that, which most doth take my *Muse*, and mee,
Is a pure cup of rich *Canary*-wine,
    Which is the *Mermaids*, now, but shall be mine:
Of which had HORACE, or ANACREON tasted,
    Their lives, as doe their lines, till now had lasted.
Tabacco, Nectar, or the *Thespian* spring,

Are all but LUTHERS beere, to this I sing.
Of this we will sup free, but moderately,
    And we will have no *Pooly'*, or *Parrot* by;
Nor shall our cups make any guiltie men:
    But, at our parting, we will be, as when
We innocently met. No simple word,
    That shall be utter'd at our mirthfull boord,
Shall make us sad next morning: or affright
    The libertie, that wee'll enjoy to night.

On Gut

Gut eates all day, and lechers all the night,
    So all his meate he tasteth over, twise:
And, striving so to double his delight,
    He makes himselfe a thorough-fare of vice.
Thus, in his belly, can he change a sin,
    Lust it comes out, that gluttony went in.

Epitaph on Salomon Pavy,
a child of Q. Elizabeths Chappel

Weepe with me all you that read
    This little storie:
And know, for whom a teare you shed,
    Death's selfe is sorry.
'Twas a child, that so did thrive
    In grace, and feature,
As *Heaven* and *Nature* seem'd to strive
    Which own'd the creature.
Yeeres he numbred scarse thirteene
    When *Fates* turn'd cruell,
Yet three fill'd *Zodiackes* had he beene
    The stages jewell;
And did act (what now we mone)
    Old men so duely,
As, sooth, the *Parcae* thought him one,
    He plai'd so truely.
So, by error, to his fate
    They all consented;
But viewing him since (alas, too late)
    They have repented.
And have sought (to give new birth)
    In bathes to steepe him;
But, being so much too good for earth,
    Heaven vowes to keepe him.

Epitaph on Elizabeth, L. H.

Would'st thou heare, what man can say
   In a little? Reader, stay.
Under-neath this stone doth lye
   As much beautie, as could dye:
Which in life did harbour give
   To more vertue, then doth live.
If, at all, shee had a fault,
   Leave it buryed in this vault.
One name was ELIZABETH,
   Th'other let it sleepe with death:
Fitter, where it dyed, to tell,
   Then that it liv'd at all. Farewell.

To his Lady, then Mrs Cary

Retyr'd, with purpose your faire worth to praise,
   'Mongst *Hampton* shades, and Phœbus grove of bayes,
I pluck'd a branch; the jealous god did frowne,
   And bad me lay th'usurped laurell downe:
Said I wrong'd him, and (which was more) his love.
   I answer'd, Daphne now no paine can prove.
Phœbus replyed. Bold head, it is not shee:
   Cary my love is, Daphne but my tree.

On the famous Voyage

No more let *Greece* her bolder fables tell
   Of HERCULES, or THESEUS going to *hell*,
ORPHEUS, ULYSSES: or the *Latine Muse*,
   With tales of *Troyes* just knight, our faiths abuse:
We have a SHELTON, and a HEYDEN got,
   Had power to act, what they to faine had not.
All, that they boast of STYX, of ACHERON,
   COCYTUS, PHLEGETON, our have prov'd in one;
The filth, stench, noyse: save only what was there
   Subtly distinguish'd, was confused here.
Their wherry had no saile, too; ours had none:
   And in it, two more horride knaves, then CHARON.
Arses were heard to croake, in stead of frogs;
   And for one CERBERUS, the whole coast was dogs.
Furies there wanted not: each scold was ten.
   And, for the cryes of *Ghosts*, women, and men,
Laden with plague-sores, and their sinnes, were heard,
   Lash'd by their consciences, to die, affeard.
Then let the former age, with this content her,
   Shee brought the *Poets* forth, but ours th'adventer.

THE VOYAGE IT SELFE

I sing the brave adventure of two wights,
And pitty 'tis, I cannot call 'hem knights:
One was; and he, for brawne, and braine, right able
To have beene stiled of King ARTHURS table.
The other was a squire, of faire degree;
But, in the action, greater man than hee:
Who gave, to take at his returne from *Hell*,
His three for one. Now, lordings, listen well.
   It was the day, what time the powerfull *Moone*
Makes the poore *Banck-side* creature wet it' shoone,

In it' owne hall; when these (in worthy scorne
Of those, that put out moneyes, on returne
From *Venice, Paris*, or some in-land passage
Of six times to, and fro, without embassage,
Of him that backward went to *Berwicke*, or which
Did dance the famous Morrisse, unto *Norwich*)
At *Bread-streets* Mermaid, having din'd, and merry,
Propos'd to goe to *Hol'borne* in a wherry:
A harder tasque, then either his to *Bristo'*,
Or his to *Antwerpe*. Therefore, once more, list ho'.
     A *Docke* there is, that called is AVERNUS,
Of some *Bride-well*, and may, in time, concerne us
All, that are readers: but, me thinkes 'tis od,
That all this while I have forgot some *god*,
Or *goddesse* to invoke, to stuffe my verse;
And with both bombard-stile, and phrase, rehearse
The many perills of this *Port*, and how
Sans helpe of SYBIL, or a golden bough,
Or magick sacrifice, they past along!
ALCIDES, be thou succouring to my song.
Thou hast seene *hell* (some say) and know'st all nookes there,
Canst tell me best, how every *Furie* lookes there,
And art a *god*, if *Fame* thee not abuses,
Always at hand, to aide the merry *Muses*.
Great *Club-fist*, though thy backe, and bones be sore,
Still, with thy former labours; yet, once more,
Act a brave worke, call it thy last adventry:
But hold my torch, while I describe the entry
To this dire passage. Say, thou stop thy nose:
'Tis but light paines: Indeede this *Dock*'s no rose.
     In the first jawes appear'd that ugly monster,
Ycleped *Mud*, which, when their oares did once stirre,
Belch'd forth an ayre, as hot, as at the muster
Of all your night-tubs, when the carts doe cluster,
Who shall discharge first his merd-urinous load:
Thorough her wombe they make their famous road,

Betweene two walls; where, on one side, to scar men,
Were seene your ugly *Centaures*, yee call Car-men,
Gorgonian scolds, and *Harpyes*: on the other
Hung stench, diseases, and old filth, their mother,
With famine, wants, and sorrowes many a dosen,
The least of which was to the plague a cosen.
But they unfrighted passe, though many a privie
Spake to 'hem louder, then the oxe in LIVIE;
And many a sinke pour'd out her rage anenst 'hem;
But still their valour, and their vertue fenc't 'hem,
And, on they went, like CASTOR brave, and POLLUX:
Ploughing the mayne. When, see (the worst of all lucks)
They met the second Prodigie, would feare a
Man, that had never heard of a *Chimaera*.
One said, it was bold BRIAREUS, or the beadle,
(Who hath the hundred hands when he doth meddle)
The other thought it HYDRA, or the rock
Made of the trull, that cut her fathers lock:
But, comming neere, they found it but a liter,
So huge, it seem'd, they could by no meanes quite her.
Backe, cry'd their brace of CHARONS: they cry'd, no,
No going backe; on still you rogues, and row.
How hight the place? a voyce was heard, COCYTUS.
Row close then, slaves. Alas, they will beshite us.
No matter, stinkards, row. What croaking sound
Is this we heare? of frogs? No, guts wind-bound,
Over your heads: Well, row. At this a loud
Crack did report it selfe, as if a cloud
Had burst with storme, and downe fell, *ab excelsis*,
Poore MERCURY, crying out on PARACELSUS,
And all his followers, that had so abus'd him:
And, in so shitten sort, so long had us'd him:
For (where he was the god of eloquence,
And subtiltie of mettalls) they dispense
His spirits, now, in pills, and eeke in potions,
Suppositories, cataplasmes, and lotions.

But many Moones there shall not wane (quoth hee)
(In the meane time, let 'hem imprison mee)
But I will speake (and know I shall be heard)
Touching this cause, where they will be affeard
To answere me. And sure, it was th'intent
Of the grave fart, late let in parliament,
Had it beene seconded, and not in fume
Vanish'd away: as you must all presume
Their MERCURY did now. By this, the stemme
Of the hulke touch'd, and, as by POLYPHEME
The slie ULYSSES stole in a sheepes-skin,
The well-greas'd wherry now had got betweene,
And bad her *fare-well sough*, unto the lurden:
Never did bottome more betray her burden;
The meate-boate of Beares colledge, *Paris-garden*,
Stunke not so ill; nor, when shee kist, KATE ARDEN.
Yet, one day in the yeere, for sweet 'tis voyc't,
And that is when it is the Lord *Maiors* foist.
     By this time had they reach'd the *Stygian* poole,
By which the *Masters* sweare, when, on the stoole
Of worship, they their nodding chinnes doe hit
Against their breasts. Here, sev'rall ghosts did flit
About the shore, of farts, but late departed,
White, black, blew, greene, and in more formes out-started,
Then all those *Atomi* ridiculous,
Whereof old DEMOCRITE, and HILL NICHOLAS,
One said, the other swore, the world consists.
These be the cause of those thicke frequent mists
Airising in that place, through which, who goes,
Must trie the'un-used valour of a nose:
And that ours did. For, yet, no nare was tainted,
Nor thumbe, nor finger to the stop acquainted,
But open, and un-arm'd encounter'd all:
Whether it languishing stucke upon the wall,
Or were precipitated downe the jakes,
And, after, swom abroad in ample flakes,

Or, that it lay, heap'd like an usurers masse,
All was to them the same, they were to passe,
And so they did, from STYX, to ACHERON:
The ever-boyling floud. Whose bankes upon
Your *Fleet*-lane *Furies*; and hot cookes doe dwell,
That, with still-scalding steemes, make the place *hell*.
The sinkes ran grease, and haire of meazled hogs,
The heads, houghs, entrails, and the hides of dogs:
For, to say truth, what scullion is so nastie,
To put the skins, and offall in a pastie?
Cats there lay divers had beene flead, and rosted,
And, after mouldie growne, againe were tosted,
Then, selling not, a dish was tane to mince 'hem,
But still, it seem'd, the ranknesse did convince 'hem.
For, here they were throwne in wi'the melted pewter,
Yet drown'd they not. They had five lives in future.
  But 'mong'st these *Tiberts*, who do'you thinke there was?
Old BANKES the juggler, our PYTHAGORAS,
Grave tutor to the learned horse. Both which,
Being, beyond sea, burned for one witch:
Their spirits transmigrated to a cat:
And, now, above the poole, a face right fat
With great gray eyes, are lifted up, and mew'd;
Thrise did it spit: thrise div'd. At last, it view'd
Our brave *Heroes* with a milder glare,
And, in a pittious tune, began. How dare
Your daintie nostrills (in so hot a season,
When every clerke eates artichokes, and peason,
Laxative lettuce, and such windie meate)
Tempt such a passage? when each privies seate
Is fill'd with buttock? And the walls doe sweate
Urine, and plaisters? when the noise doth beate
Upon your eares, of discords so un-sweet?
And out-cryes of the damned in the *Fleet*?
Cannot the *Plague*-bill keepe you backe? nor bells
Of loud SEPULCHRES with their hourely knells,

But you will visit grisly PLUTO's hall?
Behold where CERBERUS, rear'd on the wall
Of *Hol'borne* (the three sergeants heads) lookes ore,
And stayes but till you come unto the dore!
Tempt not his furie, PLUTO is away:
And MADAME CAESAR, great PROSERPINA,
Is now from home. You lose your labours quite,
Were you JOVE's sonnes, or had ALCIDES' might.
They cry'd out PUSSE. He told them he was BANKES,
That had, so often, shew'd 'hem merry prankes.
They laugh't, at his laugh-worthy fate. And past
The tripple head without a sop. At last,
Calling for RADAMANTHUS, that dwelt by,
A sope-boyler; and AEACUS him nigh,
Who kept an ale-house; with my little MINOS,
An ancient pur-blinde fletcher, with a high nose;
They tooke 'hem all to witnesse of their action:
And so went bravely backe, without protraction.
    In memorie of which most liquid deed,
The citie since hath rais'd a Pyramide.
And I could wish for their eterniz'd sakes,
My *Muse* had plough'd with his, that sung A-JAX.

THE FORREST

Why I write not of Love

Some act of *Love's* bound to reherse,
I thought to binde him, in my verse:
Which when he felt, Away (quoth hee)
Can Poets hope to fetter mee?
It is enough, they once did get
MARS, and my *Mother*, in their net:
I weare not these my wings in vaine.
With which he fled me: and againe,
Into my ri'mes could ne're be got
By any arte. Then wonder not,
That since, my numbers are so cold,
When *Love* is fled, and I grow old.

To Penshurst

Thou art not, PENSHURST, built to envious show,
  Of touch, or marble; nor canst boast a row
Of polish'd pillars, or a roofe of gold:
  Thou hast no lantherne, whereof tales are told;
Or stayre, or courts; but stand'st an ancient pile,
  And these grudg'd at, art reverenc'd the while.
Thou joy'st in better markes, of soyle, of ayre,
  Of wood, of water: therein thou art faire.
Thou hast thy walkes for health, as well as sport:
  Thy *Mount*, to which the *Dryads* doe resort,
Where PAN, and BACCHUS their high feasts have made,
  Beneath the broad beech, and the chest-nut shade;
That taller tree, which of a nut was set,
  At his great birth, where all the *Muses* met.
There, in the writhed barke, are cut the names
  Of many a SYLVANE, taken with his flames.
And thence, the ruddy *Satyres* oft provoke
  The lighter *Faunes*, to reach thy *Ladies oke*.
Thy copp's, too, nam'd of GAMAGE, thou hast there,
  That never failes to serve thee season'd deere,
When thou would'st feast, or exercise thy friends.
  The lower land, that to the river bends,
Thy sheepe, thy bullocks, kine, and calves doe feed:
  The middle grounds thy mares, and horses breed.
Each banke doth yeeld thee coneyes; and the topps
  Fertile of wood, ASHORE, and SYDNEY's copp's,
To crowne thy open table, doth provide
  The purpled pheasant, with the speckled side:
The painted partrich lyes in every field,
  And, for thy messe, is willing to be kill'd.
And if the high-swolne *Medway* faile thy dish,
  Thou hast thy ponds, that pay thee tribute fish,
Fat, aged carps, that runne into thy net.

And pikes, now weary their owne kinde to eat,
As loth, the second draught, or cast to stay,
    Officiously, at first, themselves betray.
Bright eeles, that emulate them, and leape on land,
    Before the fisher, or into his hand.
Then hath thy orchard fruit, thy garden flowers,
    Fresh as the ayre, and new as are the houres.
The earely cherry, with the later plum,
    Fig, grape, and quince, each in his time doth come:
The blushing apricot, and woolly peach
    Hang on thy walls, that every child may reach.
And though thy walls be of the countrey stone,
    They'are rear'd with no mans ruine, no mans grone,
There's none, that dwell about them, wish them downe;
    But all come in, the farmer, and the clowne:
And no one empty-handed, to salute
    Thy lord, and lady, though they have no sute.
Some bring a capon, some a rurall cake,
    Some nuts, some apples; some that thinke they make
The better cheeses, bring 'hem; or else send
    By their ripe daughters, whom they would commend
This way to husbands; and whose baskets beare
    An embleme of themselves, in plum, or peare.
But what can this (more then expresse their love)
    Adde to thy free provisions, farre above
The neede of such? whose liberall boord doth flow,
    With all, that hospitalitie doth know!
Where comes no guest, but is allow'd to eate,
    Without his feare, and of thy lords owne meate:
Where the same beere, and bread, and selfe-same wine,
    That is his Lordships, shall be also mine.
And I not faine to sit (as some, this day,
    At great mens tables) and yet dine away.
Here no man tells my cups; nor, standing by,
    A waiter, doth my gluttony envy:
But gives me what I call, and lets me eate,

He knowes, below, he shall finde plentie of meate,
Thy tables hoord not up for the next day,
    Nor, when I take my lodging, need I pray
For fire, or lights, or livorie: all is there;
    As if thou, then, wert mine, or I raign'd here:
There's nothing I can wish, for which I stay.
    That found King JAMES, when hunting late, this way,
With his brave sonne, the Prince, they saw thy fires
    Shine bright on every harth as the desires
Of thy *Penates* had beene set on flame,
    To entertayne them; or the countrey came,
With all their zeale, to warme their welcome here.
    What (great, I will not say, but) sodayne cheare
Did'st thou, then, make 'hem! and what praise was heap'd
    On thy good lady, then! who, therein, reap'd
The just reward of her high huswifery;
    To have her linnen, plate, and all things nigh,
When shee was farre: and not a roome, but drest,
    As if it had expected such a guest!
These, PENSHURST, are thy praise, and yet not all.
    Thy lady's noble, fruitfull, chaste withall.
His children thy great lord may call his owne:
    A fortune, in this age, but rarely knowne.
They are, and have beene taught religion: Thence
    Their gentler spirits have suck'd innocence.
Each morne, and even, they are taught to pray,
    With the whole houshold, and may, every day,
Reade, in their vertuous parents noble parts,
    The mysteries of manners, armes, and arts.
Now, PENSHURST, they that will proportion thee
    With other edifices, when they see
Those proud, ambitious heaps, and nothing else,
    May say, their lords have built, but thy lord dwells.

To Sir Robert Wroth

How blest art thou, canst love the countrey, WROTH,
  Whether by choice, or fate, or both;
And, though so neere the citie, and the court,
  Art tane with neithers vice, nor sport:
That at great times, art no ambitious guest
  Of Sheriffes dinner, or Maiors feast.
Nor com'st to view the better cloth of state;
  The richer hangings, or crowne-plate;
Nor throng'st (when masquing is) to have a sight
  Of the short braverie of the night;
To view the jewells, stuffes, the paines, the wit
  There wasted, some not paid for yet!
But canst, at home, in thy securer rest,
  Live, with un-bought provision blest;
Free from proud porches, or their guilded roofes,
  'Mongst loughing heards, and solide hoofes:
Along'st the curled woods, and painted meades,
  Through which a serpent river leades
To some coole, courteous shade, which he calls his,
  And makes sleepe softer then it is!
Or, if thou list the night in watch to breake,
  A-bed canst heare the loud stag speake,
In spring, oft roused for thy masters sport,
  Who, for it, makes thy house his court;
Or with thy friends, the heart of all the yeere,
  Divid'st, upon the lesser Deere;
In autumne, as the Partrich makes a flight,
  And giv'st thy gladder guests the sight;
And, in the winter, hunt'st the flying hare,
  More for thy exercise, then fare;
While all, that follow, their glad eares apply
  To the full greatnesse of the cry:
Or hauking at the river, or the bush,

Or shooting at the greedie thrush,
Thou dost with some delight the day out-weare,
   Although the coldest of the yeere!
The whil'st, the severall seasons thou hast seene
   Of flowrie fields, of cop'ces greene,
The moved meddowes, with the fleeced sheepe,
   And feasts, that either shearers keepe;
The ripened eares, yet humble in their height,
   And furrowes laden with their weight;
The apple-harvest, that doth longer last;
   The hogs return'd home fat from mast;
The trees cut out in log; and those boughes made
   A fire now, that lent a shade!
Thus PAN, and SYLVANE, having had their rites,
   COMUS puts in, for new delights;
And fills thy open hall with mirth, and cheere,
   As if in SATURNES raigne it were;
APOLLO's harpe, and HERMES lyre resound,
   Nor are the *Muses* strangers found:
The rout of rurall folke come thronging in,
   (Their rudenesse then is thought no sinne)
Thy noblest spouse affords them welcome grace;
   And the great *Heroes*, of her race,
Sit mixt with losse of state, or reverence.
   Freedome doth with degree dispense.
The jolly wassall walkes the often round,
   And in their cups, their cares are drown'd:
They thinke not, then, which side the cause shall leese,
   Nor how to get the lawyer fees.
Such, and no other was that age, of old,
   Which boasts t'have had the head of gold.
And such since thou canst make thine owne content,
   Strive, WROTH, to live long innocent.
Let others watch in guiltie armes, and stand
   The furie of a rash command,

Goe enter breaches, meet the cannons rage,
  That they may sleepe with scarres in age.
And shew their feathers shot, and cullors torne,
  And brag, that they were therefore borne.
Let this man sweat, and wrangle at the barre,
  For every price, in every jarre,
And change possessions, oftner with his breath,
  Then either money, warre, or death:
Let him, then hardest sires, more disinherit,
  And each where boast it as his merit,
To blow up orphanes, widdowes, and their states;
  And thinke his power doth equall *Fates*.
Let that goe heape a masse of wretched wealth,
  Purchas'd by rapine, worse then stealth,
And brooding o're it sit, with broadest eyes,
  Not doing good, scarce when he dyes.
Let thousands more goe flatter vice, and winne,
  By being organes to great sinne,
Get place, and honor, and be glad to keepe
  The secrets, that shall breake their sleepe:
And, so they ride in purple, eate in plate,
  Though poyson, thinke it a great fate.
But thou, my WROTH, if I can truth apply,
  Shalt neither that, not this envy:
Thy peace is made; and, when man's state is well,
  'Tis better, if he there can dwell.
God wisheth, none should wracke on a strange shelfe:
  To him, man's dearer, then t'himselfe.
And, howsoever we may thinke things sweet,
  He alwayes gives what he knowes meet;
Which who can use is happy: Such be thou.
  Thy morning's, and thy evening's vow
Be thankes to him, and earnest prayer, to finde
  A body sound, with sounder minde;

To doe thy countrey service, thy selfe right;
    That neither want doe thee affright,
Nor death; but when thy latest sand is spent,
    Thou maist thinke life, a thing but lent.

To the World

A farewell for a Gentle-woman, vertuous and noble

False world, good-night: since thou hast brought
   That houre upon my morne of age,
Hence-forth I quit thee from my thought,
   My part is ended on thy stage.
Doe not once hope, that thou canst tempt
   A spirit so resolv'd to tread
Upon thy throate, and live exempt
   From all the nets that thou canst spread.
I know thy formes are studyed arts,
   Thy subtle wayes, be narrow straits;
Thy curtesie but sodaine starts,
   And what thou call'st thy gifts are baits.
I know too, though thou strut, and paint,
   Yet art thou both shrunke up, and old,
That onely fooles make thee a saint,
   And all thy good is to be sold.
I know thou whole art but a shop
   Of toyes, and trifles, traps, and snares,
To take the weake, or make them stop:
   Yet art thou falser then thy wares.
And, knowing this, should I yet stay,
   Like such as blow away their lives,
And never will redeeme a day,
   Enamor'd of their golden gyves?
Or, having scap'd, shall I returne,
   And thrust my necke into the noose,
From whence, so lately, I did burne,
   With all my powers, my selfe to loose?
What bird, or beast, is knowne so dull,
   That fled his cage, or broke his chaine,
And tasting ayre, and freedome, wull
   Render his head in there againe?

If these, who have but sense, can shun
    The engines, that have them annoy'd;
Little, for me, had reason done,
    If I could not thy ginnes avoyd.
Yes, threaten, doe. Alas I feare
    As little, as I hope from thee:
I know thou canst nor shew, nor beare
    More hatred, then thou hast to mee.
My tender, first, and simple yeeres
    Thou did'st abuse, and then betray;
Since stird'st up jealousies and feares,
    When all the causes were away.
Then, in a soile hast planted me,
    Where breathe the basest of thy fooles;
Where envious arts professed be,
    And pride, and ignorance the schooles,
Where nothing is examin'd, weigh'd,
    But, as 'tis rumor'd, so beleev'd:
Where every freedome is betray'd
    And every goodnesse tax'd, or griev'd.
But, what we'are borne for, we must beare:
    Our fraile condition it is such,
That, what to all may happen here,
    If't chance to me, I must not grutch.
Else, I my state should much mistake,
    To harbour a divided thought
From all my kinde: that, for my sake,
    There should a miracle be wrought.
No, I doe know, that I was borne
    To age, misfortune, sicknesse, griefe:
But I will beare these, with that scorne,
    As shall not need thy false reliefe.
Nor for my peace will I goe farre,
    As wandrers doe, that still doe rome,
But make my strengths, such as they are,
    Here in my bosome, and at home.

Song. To Celia

Come my CELIA, let us prove,
While we may, the sports of love;
Time will not be ours, for ever:
He, at length, our good will sever.
Spend not then his guifts in vaine.
Sunnes, that set, may rise againe:
But if once we loose this light,
'Tis, with us, perpetuall night.
Why should we deferre our joyes?
Fame, and rumor are but toyes.
Cannot we delude the eyes
Of a few poore houshold spyes?
Or his easier eares beguile,
So removed by our wile?
'Tis no sinne, loves fruit to steale,
But the sweet theft to reveale:
To be taken, to be seene,
These have crimes accounted beene.

To the Same

Kisse me, sweet: The warie lover
Can your favours keepe, and cover,
When the common courting jay
All your bounties will betray.
Kisse againe: no creature comes.
Kisse, and score up wealthy summes
On my lips, thus hardly sundred,
While you breath. First give a hundred,
Then a thousand, then another
Hundred, then unto the tother
Adde a thousand, and so more:
Till you equall with the store,
All the grasse that *Rumney* yeelds,
Or the sands in *Chelsey* fields,
Or the drops in silver *Thames*,
Or the starres, that guild his streames,
In the silent sommer-nights,
When youths ply their stolne delights.
That the curious may not know
How to tell' hem, as they flow,
And the envious, when they find
What their number is, be pin'd.

Song. That Women are but Mens Shaddowes

Follow a shaddow, it still flies you;
    Seeme to flye it, it will pursue:
So court a mistris, shee denyes you;
    Let her alone, shee will court you.
Say, are not women truely, then,
    Stil'd but the shaddowes of us men?
At morne, and even, shades are longest;
    At noone, they are or short, or none:
So men at weakest, they are strongest,
    But grant us perfect, they're not knowne.
Say, are not women truely, then,
    Stil'd but the shaddowes of us men?

Song. To Celia

Drinke to me, onely, with thine eyes,
   And I will pledge with mine;
Or leave a kisse but in the cup,
   And Ile not looke for wine.
The thirst, that from the soule doth rise,
   Doth aske a drinke divine:
But might I of JOVE's *Nectar* sup,
   I would not change for thine.
I sent thee, late, a rosie wreath,
   Not so much honoring thee,
As giving it a hope, that there
   It could not withered bee.
But thou thereon did'st onely breath,
   And sent'st it backe to mee:
Since when it growes, and smells, I sweare,
   Not of it selfe, but thee.

'Not to know vice at all . . .'

Not to know vice at all, and keepe true state,
    Is vertue, and not *Fate*:
Next, to that vertue, is to know vice well,
    And her blacke spight expell.
Which to effect (since no brest is so sure,
    Or safe, but shee'll procure
Some way of entrance) we must plant a guard
    Of thoughts to watch, and ward
At th'eye and eare (the ports unto the minde)
    That no strange, or unkinde
Object arrive there, but the heart (our spie)
    Give knowledge instantly,
To wakefull reason, our affections king:
    Who (in th'examining)
Will quickly taste the treason, and commit
    Close, the close cause of it.
'Tis the securest policie we have,
    To make our sense our slave.
But this true course is not embrac'd by many:
    By many? scarse by any.
For either our affections doe rebell,
    Or else the sentinell
(That should ring larum to the heart) doth sleepe,
    Or some great thought doth keepe
Backe the intelligence, and falsely sweares,
    Th'are base, and idle feares
Whereof the loyall conscience so complaines.
    Thus, by these subtle traines,
Doe severall passions still invade the minde,
    And strike our reason blinde.
Of which usurping rancke, some have thought love
    The first; as prone to move

Most frequent tumults, horrors, and unrests,
    In our enflamed brests:
But this doth from their cloud of error grow,
    Which thus we over-blow.
The thing, they here call Love, is blinde Desire,
    Arm'd with bow, shafts, and fire;
Inconstant, like the sea, of whence 'tis borne,
    Rough, swelling, like a storme:
With whom who sailes, rides on the surge of feare,
    And boyles, as if he were
In a continuall tempest. Now, true Love
    No such effects doth prove;
That is an essence, farre more gentle, fine,
    Pure, perfect, nay divine;
It is a golden chaine let downe from heaven,
    Whose linkes are bright, and even,
That falls like sleepe on lovers, and combines
    The soft, and sweetest mindes
In equall knots: This beares no brands, nor darts,
    To murther different hearts,
But, in a calme, and god-like unitie,
    Preserves communitie.
O, who is he, that (in this peace) enjoyes
    The' *Elixir* of all joyes?
A forme more fresh, then are the *Eden* bowers,
    And lasting, as her flowers:
Richer then *Time*, and as *Time's* vertue, rare.
    Sober, as saddest care:
A fixed thought, an eye un-taught to glance;
    Who (blest with such high chance)
Would, at suggestion of a steepe desire,
    Cast himselfe from the spire
Of all his happinesse? But soft: I heare
    Some vicious foole draw neare,
That cryes, we dreame, and sweares, there's no such thing,
    As this chaste love we sing.

Peace, Luxurie, thou are like one of those
    Who, being at sea, suppose,
Because they move, the continent doth so:
    No, vice, we let thee know,
Though thy wild thoughts with sparrowes wings doe flye,
    Turtles can chastly dye;
And yet (in this t'expresse our selves more cleare)
    We doe not number, here,
Such spirits as are onely continent,
    Because lust's meanes are spent:
Or those, who doubt the common mouth of fame,
    And for their place, and name,
Cannot so safely sinne. Their chastitie
    Is meere necessitie.
Nor meane we those, whom vowes and conscience
    Have fill'd with abstinence:
Though we acknowledge, who can so abstayne,
    Makes a most blessed gayne.
He that for love of goodnesse hateth ill,
    Is more crowne-worthy still,
Then he, which for sinnes penaltie forbeares.
    His heart sinnes, though he feares.
But we propose a person like our Dove,
    Grac'd with a Phœnix love;
A beautie of that cleere, and sparkling light,
    Would make a day of night,
And turne the blackest sorrowes to bright joyes:
    Whose od'rous breath destroyes
All taste of bitternesse, and makes the ayre
    As sweet, as shee is fayre.
A body so harmoniously compos'd,
    As if *Nature* disclos'd
All her best symmetrie in that one feature!
    O, so divine a creature
Who could be false to? chiefly, when he knowes
    How onely shee bestowes

The wealthy treasure of her love on him;
    Making his fortunes swim
In the full floud of her admir'd perfection?
    What savage, brute affection,
Would not be fearfull to offend a dame
    Of this excelling frame?
Much more a noble, and right generous mind
    (To vertuous moods inclin'd)
That knowes the waight of guilt: He will refraine
    From thoughts of such a straine.
And to his sense object this sentence ever,
    Man may securely sinne, but safely never.

Ode. To Sir William Sydney, on his Birth-day

Now that the harth is crown'd with smiling fire,
  And some doe drinke, and some doe dance,
        Some ring,
        Some sing,
  And all doe strive t'advance
The gladnesse higher:
    Wherefore should I
    Stand silent by,
      Who not the least,
      Both love the cause, and authors of the feast?
Give me my cup, but from the *Thespian* well,
  That I may tell to SYDNEY, what
        This day
        Doth say,
  And he may thinke on that
Which I doe tell:
    When all the noyse
    Of these forc'd joyes,
      Are fled and gone,
      And he, with his best *Genius* left alone.
This day sayes, then, the number of glad yeeres
  Are justly summ'd, that make you man;
        Your vow
        Must now
  Strive all right wayes it can,
T'out-strip your peeres:
    Since he doth lacke
    Of going backe
      Little, whose will
      Doth urge him to runne wrong, or to stand still.
Nor can a little of the common store,
  Of nobles vertue, shew in you;
        Your blood

             So good
        And great, must seeke for new,
    And studie more:
        Not weary, rest
        On what's deceast.
            For they, that swell
            With dust of ancestors, in graves but dwell.
'T will be exacted of your name, whose sonne,
    Whose nephew, whose grand-child you are;
                And men
                Will, then,
        Say you have follow'd farre,
    When well begunne:
        Which must be now,
        They teach you, how.
            And he that stayes
            To live until to morrow' hath lost two dayes.
So may you live in honor, as in name,
    If with this truth you be inspir'd,
                So may
                This day
        Be more, and long desir'd:
    And with the flame
        Of love be bright,
        As with the light
            Of bone-fires. Then
            The Birth-day shines, when logs not burne, but men.

To Heaven

Good, and great GOD, can I not thinke of thee,
    But it must, straight, my melancholy bee?
Is it interpreted in me disease,
    That, laden with my sinnes, I seeke for ease?
O, be thou witnesse, that the reynes dost know,
    And hearts of all, if I be sad for show,
And judge me after: if I dare pretend
    To ought but grace, or ayme at other end.
As thou art all, so be thou all to mee,
    First, midst, and last, converted one, and three;
My faith, my hope, my love: and in this state,
    My judge, my witnesse, and my advocate.
Where have I beene this while exil'd from thee?
    And whither rap'd, now thou but stoup'st to mee?
Dwell, dwell here still: O, being every-where,
    How can I doubt to finde thee ever, here?
I know my state, both full of shame, and scorne,
    Conceiv'd in sinne, and unto labour borne,
Standing with feare, and must with horror fall,
    And destin'd unto judgement, after all.
I feele my griefes too, and there scarce is ground,
    Upon my flesh t'inflict another wound.
Yet dare I not complaine, or wish for death
    With holy PAUL, lest it be thought the breath
Of discontent; or that these prayers bee
    For wearinesse of life, not love of thee.

THE UNDER-WOOD

A Celebration of Charis
in ten Lyrick Peeces

1. HIS EXCUSE FOR LOVING

Let it not your wonder move,
Lesse your laughter; that I love.
Though I now write fiftie yeares,
I have had, and have my Peeres;
Poëts, though divine, are men:
Some have lov'd as old agen.
And it is not alwayes face,
Clothes, or Fortune gives the grace;
Or the feature, or the youth:
But the Language, and the Truth,
With the Ardor, and the Passion,
Gives the Lover weight, and fashion.
If you then will read the Storie,
First, prepare you to be sorie,
That you never knew till now,
Either whom to love, or how:
But be glad, as soone with me,
When you know, that this is she,
Of whose Beautie it was sung,
She shall make the old man young,
Keepe the middle age at stay,
And let nothing high decay,
Till she be the reason why,
All the world for love may die.

2. HOW HE SAW HER

I beheld her on a day,
When her looke out-flourisht May:
And her dressing did out-brave
All the Pride the fields than have:

Farre I was from being stupid,
For I ran and call'd on *Cupid*;
Love, if thou wilt ever see
Marke of glorie, come with me;
Where's thy Quiver? bend thy Bow:
Here's a shaft, thou are to slow!
And (withall) I did untie
Every Cloud about his eye;
But, he had not gain'd his sight
Sooner, then he lost his might,
Or his courage; for away
Strait hee ran, and durst not stay,
Letting Bow and Arrow fall,
Nor for any threat, or call,
Could be brought once back to looke.
I foole-hardie, there up-tooke
Both the Arrow he had quit,
And the Bow: with thought to hit
This my object. But she threw
Such a Lightning (as I drew)
At my face, that tooke my sight,
And my motion from me quite;
So that, there, I stood a stone,
Mock'd of all: and call'd of one
(Which with griefe and wrath I heard)
Cupids Statue with a Beard,
Or else one that plaid his Ape,
In a *Hercules*-his shape.

3. What hee suffered

After many scornes like these,
Which the prouder Beauties please,
She content was to restore
Eyes and limbes; to hurt me more.
And would on Conditions, be

Reconcil'd to Love, and me.
First, that I must kneeling yeeld
Both the Bow, and shaft I held,
Unto her; which Love might take
At her hand, with oath, to make
Mee, the scope of his next draught,
Aymed with that selfe-same shaft.
He no sooner heard the Law,
But the Arrow home did draw
And (to gaine her by his Art)
Left it sticking in my heart:
Which when she beheld to bleed,
She repented of the deed,
And would faine have chang'd the fate,
But the Pittie comes too late.
Looser-like, now, all my wreake
Is, that I have leave to speake,
And in either Prose, or Song,
To revenge me with my Tongue,
Which how Dexterously I doe,
Heare and make Example too.

4. Her Triumph

See the Chariot at hand here of Love,
    Wherein my Lady rideth!
Each that drawes, is a Swan, or a Dove,
    And well the Carre Love guideth.
As she goes, all hearts doe duty
                Unto her beauty;
And enamour'd, doe wish, so they might
                But enjoy such a sight,
That they still were to run by her side,
Thorough Swords, thorough Seas, whether she would ride.

Doe but looke on her eyes, they doe light
    All that Loves world compriseth!

Doe but looke on her Haire, it is bright
    As Loves starre when it riseth!
Doe but marke, her forehead's smoother
                    Then words that sooth her!
And from her arched browes, such a grace
                    Sheds it selfe through the face,
    As alone there triumphs to the life
All the Gaine, all the Good, of the Elements strife.

Have you seene but a bright Lillie grow,
    Before rude hands have touch'd it?
Have you mark'd but the fall o'the Snow
    Before the soyle hath smutch'd it?
Have you felt the wooll o' the Bever?
                    Or Swans Downe ever?
Or have smelt o'the bud o'the Brier?
                    Or the Nard i' the fire?
    Or have tasted the bag o'the Bee?
O so white! O so soft! O so sweet is she!

5. His discourse with Cupid

Noblest *Charis*, you that are
Both my fortune, and my Starre!
And doe governe more my blood,
Then the various Moone the flood!
Heare, what late Discourse of you,
Love, and I have had; and true.
'Mongst my Muses finding me,
Where he chanc't your name to see
Set, and to this softer straine;
Sure, said he, if I have Braine,
This, here sung, can be no other
By description, but my Mother!
So hath *Homer* prais'd her haire;
So, *Anacreon* drawne the Ayre
Of her face, and made to rise,

Just above her sparkling eyes,
Both her Browes, bent like my Bow.
By her lookes I doe her know,
Which you call my Shafts. And see!
Such my Mothers blushes be,
As the Bath your verse discloses
In her cheekes, of Milke, and Roses;
Such as oft I wanton in!
And, above her even chin,
Have you plac'd the banke of kisses,
Where, you say, men gather blisses,
Rip'ned with a breath more sweet,
Then when flowers, and West-winds meet.
Nay, her white and polish'd neck,
With the Lace that doth it deck,
Is my Mothers! Hearts of slaine
Lovers, made into a Chaine!
And betweene each rising breast,
Lyes the Valley, cal'd my nest,
Where I sit and proyne my wings
After flight; and put new stings
To my shafts! Her very Name,
With my Mothers is the same.
I confesse all, I replide,
And the Glasse hangs by her side,
And the Girdle 'bout her waste,
All is *Venus*: save unchaste.
But alas, thou seest the least
Of her good, who is the best
Of her Sex; But could'st thou, *Love*,
Call to mind the formes, that strove
For the Apple, and those three
Make in one, the same were shee.
For this Beauty yet doth hide
Something more then thou hast spi'd.
Outward Grace weake love beguiles:

Shee is *Venus*, when she smiles,
But shee's *Juno*, when she walkes,
And *Minerva*, when she talkes.

6. CLAYMING A SECOND KISSE BY DESERT

Charis, guesse, and doe not misse,
Since I drew a Morning kisse
From your lips, and suck'd an ayre
Thence, as sweet, as you are faire,
    What my Muse and I have done:
Whether we have lost, or wonne,
If by us, the oddes were laid,
That the Bride (allow'd a Maid)
Look'd not halfe so fresh, and faire,
With th'advantage of her haire,
And her Jewels, to the view
Of th'Assembly, as did you!
    Or, that did you sit, or walke,
You were more the eye, and talke
Of the Court, to day, then all
Else that glister'd in *White-hall*;
So, as those that had your sight,
Wisht the Bride were chang'd to night,
And did thinke, such Rites were due
To no other Grace but you!
    Or, if you did move to night
In the Daunces, with what spight
Of your Peeres, you were beheld,
That at every motion sweld
So to see a Lady tread,
As might all the Graces lead,
And was worthy (being so seene)
To be envi'd of the Queene.
Or if you would yet have stay'd,
Whether any would up-braid

To himselfe his losse of Time;
Or have charg'd his sight of Crime,
To have left all sight for you:
 Guesse of these, which is the true;
And, if such a verse as this,
May not claime another kisse.

7. BEGGING ANOTHER, ON COLOUR OF MENDING THE FORMER

For *Loves*-sake, kisse me once againe,
 I long, and should not beg in vaine,
 Here's none to spie, or see;
  Why doe you doubt, or stay?
 I'le taste as lightly as the Bee,
That doth but touch his flower, and flies away.
 Once more, and (faith) I will be gone,
 Can he that loves, aske lesse then one?
  Nay, you may erre in this,
   And all your bountie wrong:
 This could be call'd but halfe a kisse.
What w'are but once to doe, we should doe long.
 I will but mend the last, and tell
 Where, how it would have relish'd well;
  Joyne lip to lip, and try:
   Each suck the others breath.
 And whilst our tongues perplexed lie,
Let who will thinke us dead, or wish our death.

8. URGING HER OF A PROMISE

Charis one day in discourse
Had of Love, and of his force,
Lightly promis'd, she would tell
What a man she could love well:
And that promise set on fire
All that heard her, with desire.

With the rest, I long expected,
When the worke would be effected:
But we find that cold delay,
And excuse spun every day,
As, untill she tell her one,
We all feare, she loveth none.
Therefore, *Charis*, you must do't,
For I will so urge you to't,
You shall neither eat, nor sleepe,
No, nor forth your window peepe,
With your emissarie eye,
To fetch in the Formes goe by:
And pronounce, which band, or lace,
Better fits him, then his face;
Nay, I will not let you sit
'Fore your Idoll Glasse a whit,
To say over every purle
There; or to reforme a curle;
Or with Secretarie *Sis*
To consult, if *Fucus* this
Be as good, as was the last:
All your sweet of life is past,
Make accompt, unlesse you can,
(And that quickly) speake your Man.

9. HER MAN DESCRIBED BY HER OWNE DICTAMEN

Of your Trouble, *Ben*, to ease me,
I will tell what Man would please me.
I would have him, if I could,
Noble; or of greater Blood:
Titles, I confesse, doe take me;
And a woman God did make me:
French to boote, at least in fashion,
And his Manners of that Nation.

    Young I'ld have him too, and faire,

Yet a man; with crisped haire
Cast in thousand snares, and rings
For *Loves* fingers, and his wings:
Chestnut colour, or more slack
Gold, upon a ground of black.
Venus, and *Minerva's* eyes,
For he must looke wanton-wise.

    Eye-brows bent like *Cupids* bow,
Front, an ample field of snow;
Even nose, and cheeke (withall)
Smooth as is the Billiard Ball:
Chin, as woolly as the Peach;
And his lip should kissing teach,
Till he cherish'd too much beard,
And make *Love* or me afeard.

    He would have a hand as soft
As the Downe, and shew it oft;
Skin as smooth as any rush,
And so thin, to see a blush
Rising through it e're it came;
All his blood should be a flame
Quickly fir'd, as in beginners
In loves schoole, and yet no sinners.

    'Twere too long, to speake of all:
What we harmonie doe call
In a body, should be there.
Well he should his clothes too weare;
Yet no Taylor help to make him;
Drest, you still for man should take him;
And not thinke h'had eat a stake,
Or were set up in a Brake.

    Valiant he should be as fire,
Shewing danger more then ire.
Bounteous as the clouds to earth;
And as honest as his Birth.
All his actions to be such,

As to doe no thing too much.
Nor o're-praise, nor yet condemne;
Nor out-valew, nor contemne;
Nor doe wrongs, nor wrongs receave;
Nor tie knots, nor knots unweave;
And from basenesse to be free,
As he durst love Truth and me.

  Such a man, with every part,
I could give my very heart;
But of one, if short he came,
I can rest me where I am.

10. ANOTHER LADYES EXCEPTION
PRESENT AT THE HEARING

For his Mind, I doe not care,
That's a Toy, that I could spare:
Let his Title be but great,
His Clothes rich, and band sit neat,
Himselfe young, and face be good,
All I wish is understood.
What you please, you parts may call,
'Tis one good part I'ld lie withall.

A Song

Oh doe not wanton with those eyes,
  Lest I be sick with seeing;
Nor cast them downe, but let them rise,
  Lest shame destroy their being.
O, be not angry with those fires,
  For then their threats will kill me;
Nor looke too kind on my desires,
  For then my hopes will spill me.
O, doe not steepe them in thy Teares,
  For so will sorrow slay me;
Nor spread them as distract with feares,
  Mine owne enough betray me.

In the person of Woman-kind
A Song Apologetique

Men, if you love us, play no more
  The fooles, or Tyrants with your friends,
To make us still sing o're, and o're,
    Our owne false praises, for your ends:
      Wee have both wits, and fancies too,
      And if wee must, let's sing of you.

Nor doe we doubt, but that we can,
  If wee would search with care, and paine,
Find some one good, in some one man;
    So going thorow all your straine,
      Wee shall, at last, of parcells make
      One good enough for a songs sake.

And as a cunning Painter takes
  In any curious peece you see
More pleasure while the thing he makes
    Then when 'tis made, why so will wee.
      And having pleas'd our art, wee'll try
      To make a new, and hang that by.

Another. In defence of their Inconstancie
A Song

Hang up those dull, and envious fooles,
　That talke abroad of Womans change,
We were not bred to sit on stooles,
　　Our proper vertue is to range:
　　　Take that away, you take our lives,
　　　We are no women then, but wives.

Such as in valour would excell,
　Doe change, though man, and often fight,
Which we in love must doe aswell,
　　If ever we will love aright.
　　　The frequent varying of the deed,
　　　Is that which doth perfection breed.

Nor is't inconstancie to change
　For what is better, or to make
(By searching) what before was strange,
　　Familiar, for the uses sake;
　　　The good, from bad, is not descride,
　　　But as 'tis often vext and tri'd.

And this profession of a store
　In love, doth not alone help forth
Our pleasure; but preserves us more
　　From being forsaken, then doth worth:
　　　For were the worthiest woman curst
　　　To love one man, hee'd leave her first.

The Houre-glasse

Doe but consider this small dust,
Here running in the Glasse,
  By Atomes mov'd;
Could you beleeve, that this,
  The body ever was
    Of one that lov'd?
And in his Mistress flame, playing like a flye,
  Turn'd to cinders by her eye?
  Yes; and in death, as life, unblest,
    To have't exprest,
  Even ashes of lovers find no rest.

My Picture left in *Scotland*

I now thinke, Love is rather deafe, then blind,
  For else it could not be,
    That she,
Whom I adore so much, should so slight me,
 And cast my love behind:
I'm sure my language to her, was as sweet,
   And every close did meet
   In sentence, of as subtile feet,
    As hath the youngest Hee,
 That sits in shadow of *Apollo's* tree.

Oh, but my conscious feares,
   That flie my thoughts betweene,
   Tell me that she hath seene
   My hundred of gray haires,
   Told seven and fortie years,
 Read so much wast, as she cannot imbrace
  My mountaine belly, and my rockie face,
And all these through her eyes, have stopt her eares.

Against Jealousie

Wretched and foolish Jealousie,
How cam'st thou thus to enter me?
     I ne're was of thy kind;
   Nor have I yet the narrow mind
     To vent that poore desire,
That others should not warme them at my fire,
     I wish the Sun should shine
On all mens Fruit, and flowers, as well as mine.

But under the Disguise of love,
Thou sai'st, thou only cam'st to prove
     What my Affections were.
   Think'st thou that love is help'd by feare?
     Goe, get thee quickly forth,
Loves sicknesse, and his noted want of worth,
     Seeke doubting Men to please,
I ne're will owe my health to a disease.

The Dreame

Or Scorne, or pittie on me take,
I must the true Relation make,
    I am undone to night;
  Love in a subtile Dreame disguis'd,
  Hath both my heart and me surpriz'd,
Whom never yet he durst attempt awake;
Nor will he tell me for whose sake
            He did me the Delight,
                    Or Spight,
  But leaves me to inquire,
  In all my wild desire,
    Of sleepe againe, who was his Aid;
    And sleepe so guiltie and afraid,
As since he dares not come within my sight.

An Epitaph on Master Vincent Corbet

I have my Pietie too, which could
It vent it selfe, but as it would,
   Would say as much, as both have done
   Before me here, the Friend and Sonne;
For I both lost a friend and Father,
Of him whose bones this Grave doth gather:
   Deare *Vincent Corbet*, who so long
   Had wrestled with Diseases strong,
That though they did possesse each limbe,
Yet he broke them, e're they could him,
   With the just Canon of his life,
   A life that knew nor noise, nor strife:
But was by sweetning so his will,
All order, and Disposure, still.
   His Mind as pure, and neatly kept,
   As were his Nourceries; and swept
So of uncleannesse, or offence,
That never came ill odour thence:
   And adde his Actions unto these,
   They were as specious as his Trees.
'Tis true, he could not reprehend;
His very Manners taught t'amend,
   They were so even, grave, and holy;
   No stubbornnesse so stiffe, nor folly
To licence ever was so light,
As twice to trespasse in his sight,
   His lookes would so correct it, when
   It chid the vice, yet not the Men.
Much from him I professe I wonne,
And more, and more, I should have done,
   But that I understood him scant.
   Now I conceive him by my want,
And pray who shall my sorrowes read,

That they for me their teares will shed;
   For truly, since he left to be,
   I feele, I'm rather dead than he!

Reader, whose life, and name, did e're become
   An *Epitaph*, deserv'd a *Tombe*:
Nor wants it here through penurie, or sloth,
   Who makes the *one*, so't be first, makes *both*.

An Elegie

Though Beautie be the Marke of praise,
  And yours of whom I sing be such
  As not the World can praise too much,
Yet is't your vertue now I raise.

A vertue, like Allay, so gone
  Throughout your forme; as though that move,
  And draw, and conquer all mens love,
This subjects you to love of one.

Wherein you triumph yet: because
  'Tis of your selfe, and that you use
  The noblest freedome, not to chuse
Against or Faith, or honours lawes.

But who should lesse expect from you,
  In whom alone Love lives agen?
  By whom he is restor'd to men:
And kept, and bred, and brought up true.

His falling Temples you have rear'd,
  The withered Garlands tane away;
  His Altars kept from the Decay,
That envie wish'd, and Nature fear'd.

And on them burne so chaste a flame,
  With so much Loyalties expence,
  As Love, t'aquit such excellence,
Is gone himselfe into your Name.

And you are he: the Dietie
  To whom all Lovers are design'd,
  That would their better objects find:
Among which faithful troope am I.

Who as an off'ring at your shrine,
   Have sung this Hymne, and here intreat
   One sparke of your Diviner heat
To light upon a Love of mine.

Which if it kindle not, but scant
   Appeare, and that to shortest view,
   Yet give me leave t'adore in you
What I, in her, am griev'd to want.

An Ode. To himselfe

Where do'st thou carelesse lie,
  Buried in ease and sloth?
Knowledge, that sleepes, doth die;
And this Securitie,
  It is the common Moath,
That eats on wits, and Arts, and oft destroyes them both.

Are all th'*Aonian* springs
  Dri'd up? lyes *Thespia* wast?
Doth *Clarius* Harp want strings,
That not a Nymph now sings?
  Or droop they as disgrac't,
To see their Seats and Bowers by chattring Pies defac't?

If hence thy silence be,
  As 'tis too just a cause;
Let this thought quicken thee,
Minds that are great and free,
  Should not on fortune pause,
'Tis crowne enough to vertue still, her owne applause.

What though the greedie Frie
  Be taken with false Baytes
Of worded Balladrie,
And thinke it Poësie?
  They die with their conceits,
And only pitious scorne, upon their folly waites.

Then take in hand thy Lyre,
  Strike in thy proper straine,
With *Japhets* lyne, aspire
Sols Chariot for new fire,
  To give the world againe:
Who aided him, will thee, the issue of *Joves* braine.

And since our Daintie age,
    Cannot indure reproofe,
Make not thy selfe a Page,
To that strumpet the Stage,
    But sing high and aloofe,
Safe from the wolves black jaw, and the dull Asses hoofe.

A Fit of Rime against Rime

Rime, the rack of finest wits,
That expresseth but by fits,
                       True Conceipt,
Spoyling Senses of their Treasure,
Cosening Judgement with a measure,
                       But false weight.
Wresting words, from their true calling;
Propping Verse, for feare of falling
                       To the ground.
Joynting Syllabes, drowning Letters,
Fastning Vowells, as with fetters
                       They were bound!
Soone as lazie thou wert knowne,
All good Poëtrie hence was flowne,
                       And Art banish'd.
For a thousand yeares together,
All *Parnassus* Greene did wither,
                       And wit vanish'd.
Pegasus did flie away,
At the Well no Muse did stay,
                       But bewailed
So to see the Fountaine drie,
And *Apollo's* Musique die,
                       All light failed!
Starveling rimes did fill the Stage,
Not a Poët in an Age,
                       Worth a crowning.
Not a worke deserving Baies,
Nor a lyne deserving praise,
                       Pallas frowning.
Greeke was free from Rimes infection,
Happy Greeke, by this protection,
                       Was not spoyled.

Whilst the Latin, Queene of Tongues,
Is not yet free from Rimes wrongs,
                              But rests foiled.
Scarce the Hill againe doth flourish,
Scarce the world a Wit doth nourish,
                              To restore
Phœbus to his Crowne againe;
And the Muses to their braine;
                              As before.
Vulgar Languages that want
Words, and sweetnesse, and be scant
                              Of true measure,
Tyran Rime hath so abused,
That they long since have refused
                              Other ceasure.
He that first invented thee,
May his joynts tormented bee,
                              Cramp'd for ever;
Still may Syllabes jarre with time,
Stil may reason warre with rime,
                              Resting never.
May his Sense, when it would meet
The cold tumour in his feet,
                              Grow unsounder.
And his Title be long foole,
That in rearing such a Schoole,
                              Was the founder.

An Epitaph (On Elizabeth Chute)

What Beautie would have lovely stilde,
What manners prettie, Nature milde,
What wonder perfect, all were fil'd,
Upon record, in this blest child.
   And, till the comming of the Soule
   To fetch the flesh, we keepe the Rowle.

An Elegie

'Tis true, I'm broke! Vowes, Oathes, and all I had
    Of Credit lost. And I am now run madde:
Or doe upon my selfe some desperate ill;
    This sadnesse makes no approaches, but to kill.
It is a Darknesse hath blockt up my sense,
    And drives it in to eat on my offence,
Or there to sterve it. Helpe, O you that may
    Alone lend succours, and this furie stay,
Offended Mistris, you are yet so faire,
    As light breakes from you, that affrights despaire,
And fills my powers with perswading joy,
    That you should be too noble to destroy.
There may some face or menace of a storme
    Looke forth, but cannot last in such a forme.
If there be nothing worthy you can see
    Of Graces, or your mercie here in me,
Spare your owne goodnesse yet; and be not great
    In will and power, only to defeat.
God, and the good, know to forgive, and save.
    The ignorant, and fooles, no pittie have.
I will not stand to justifie my fault,
    Or lay the excuse upon the Vintners vault;
Or in confessing of the Crime be nice,
    Or goe about to countenance the vice,
By naming in what companie 'twas in,
    As I would urge Authoritie for sinne.
No, I will stand arraign'd, and cast, to be
    The Subject of your Grace in pardoning me,
And (stil'd your mercies Creature) will live more
    Your honour now, then your disgrace before.
Thinke it was frailtie, Mistris, thinke me man,
    Thinke that your selfe like heaven forgive me can:
Where weaknesse doth offend, and vertue grieve,

There greatnesse takes a glorie to relieve.
Thinke that I once was yours, or may be now;
    Nothing is vile, that is a part of you:
Errour and folly in me may have crost
    Your just commands; yet those, not I, be lost.
I am regenerate now, become the child
    Of your compassion; Parents should be mild:
There is no Father that for one demerit,
    Or two, or three, a Sonne will dis-inherit,
That as the last of punishments is meant;
    No man inflicts that paine, till hope be spent:
An ill-affected limbe (what e're it aile)
    We cut not off, till all Cures else doe faile:
And then with pause; for sever'd once, that's gone,
    Would live his glory that could keepe it on;
Doe not despaire my mending; to distrust
    Before you prove a medicine, is unjust.
You may so place me, and in such an ayre,
    As not alone the Cure, but scarre be faire.
That is, if still your Favours you apply,
    And not the bounties you ha' done deny.
Could you demand the gifts you gave, againe?
    Why was't? did e're the Cloudes aske back their raine?
The Sunne his heat, and light, the ayre his dew?
    Or winds the Spirit, by which the flower so grew?
That were to wither all, and make a Grave
    Of that wise Nature would a Cradle have.
Her order is to cherish, and preserve,
    Consumptions nature to destroy, and sterve.
But to exact againe what once is given,
    Is natures meere obliquitie! as Heaven
Should aske the blood, and spirits he hath infus'd
    In man, because man hath the flesh abus'd.
O may your wisdome take example hence,
    God lightens not at mans each fraile offence,
He pardons slips, goes by a world of ills,

And then his thunder frights more, then it kills.
He cannot angrie be, but all must quake,
    It shakes even him, that all things else doth shake.
And how more faire, and lovely lookes the world
    In a calme skie, then when the heaven is horl'd
About in Cloudes, and wrapt in raging weather,
    As all with storme and tempest ran together.
O imitate that sweet Serenitie
    That makes us live, not that which calls to die.
In darke, and sullen mornes, doe we not say,
    This looketh like an Execution day?
And with the vulgar doth it not obtaine
    The name of Cruell weather, storme, and raine?
Be not affected with these markes too much
    Of crueltie, lest they doe make you such.
But view the mildnesse of your Makers state,
    As I the penitents here emulate:
He when he sees a sorrow such as this,
    Streight puts off all his Anger, and doth kisse
The contrite Soule, who hath no thought to win
    Upon the hope to have another sin
Forgiven him; And in that lyne stand I,
    Rather then once displease you more, to die,
To suffer tortures, scorne, and Infamie,
    What Fooles, and all their Parasites can apply;
The wit of Ale, and *Genius* of the Malt
    Can pumpe for; or a Libell without salt
Produce; though threatning with a coale, or chalke
    On every wall, and sung where e're I walke.
I number these as being of the Chore
    Of Contumelie, and urge a good man more
Then sword, or fire, or what is of the race
    To carry noble danger in the face:
There is not any punishment, or paine,
    A man should flie from, as he would disdaine.
Then Mistris, here, here let your rigour end,

And let your mercie make me asham'd to offend.
I will no more abuse my vowes to you,
   Then I will studie falshood, to be true.
O, that you could but by dissection see
   How much you are the better part of me;
How all my Fibres by your Spirit doe move,
   And that there is no life in me, but love.
You would be then most confident, that tho
   Publike affaires command me now to goe
Out of your eyes, and be awhile away;
   Absence, or Distance, shall not breed decay.
Your forme shines here, here fixed in my heart:
   I may dilate my selfe, but not depart.
Others by common Stars their courses run,
   When I see you, then I doe see my Sun,
Till then 'tis all but darknesse, that I have;
   Rather then want your light, I wish a grave.

An Elegie

That Love's a bitter sweet, I ne're conceive
    Till the sower Minute comes of taking leave,
And then I taste it. But as men drinke up
    In hast the bottome of a med'cin'd Cup,
And take some sirrup after; so doe I,
    To put all relish from my memorie
Of parting, drowne it in the hope to meet
    Shortly againe: and make our absence sweet.
This makes me, Mistress that sometime by stealth,
    Under another Name, I take your health;
And turne the Ceremonies of those Nights
    I give, or owe my friends, into your Rites,
But ever without blazon, or least shade
    Of vowes so sacred, and in silence made;
For though Love thrive, and may grow up with cheare,
    And free societie, hee's borne else-where,
And must be bred, so to conceale his birth,
    As neither wine doe rack it out, or mirth.
Yet should the Lover still be ayrie and light,
    In all his Actions rarified to spright;
Not, like a *Midas*, shut up in himselfe,
    And turning all he toucheth into pelfe,
Keepe in reserv'd in his Dark-lanterne face,
    As if that ex'lent Dulnesse were Loves grace;
No, Mistris, no, the open merrie Man
    Moves like a sprightly River, and yet can
Keepe secret in his Channels what he breedes,
    'Bove all your standing waters, choak'd with weedes.
They looke at best like Creame-bowles, and you soone
    Shall find their depth: they're sounded with a spoone
They may say Grace, and for Loves Chaplaines passe;
    But the grave Lover ever was an Asse;
Is fix'd upon one leg, and dares not come

Out with the other, for hee's still at home;
Like the dull wearied Crane that (come on land)
   Doth, while he keepes his watch, betray his stand.
Where he that knowes will, like a Lapwing, flie
   Farre from the Nest, and so himselfe belie
To others, as he will deserve the Trust
   Due to that one, that doth believe him just.
And such your Servant is, who vowes to keepe
   The Jewell of your name, as close as sleepe
Can lock the Sense up, or the heart a thought,
   And never be by time, or folly brought,
Weaknesse of braine, or any charme of Wine,
   The sinne of Boast, or other countermine
(Made to blow up loves secrets) to discover
   That Article, may not become your lover:
Which in assurance to your brest I tell,
   If I had writ no word, but Deare, farewell.

An Elegie

Since you must goe, and I must bid farewell,
    Heare, Mistris, your departing servant tell
What it is like: And doe not thinke they can
    Be idle words, though of a parting Man;
It is as if a night should shade noone-day,
    Or that the Sun was here, but forc't away;
And we were left under that Hemisphere,
    Where we must feele it Darke for halfe a yeare.
What fate is this, to change mens dayes and houres,
    To shift their seasons, and destroy their powers!
Alas I ha' lost my heat, my blood, my prime,
    Winter is come a Quarter e're his Time,
My health will leave me; and when you depart,
    How shall I doe, sweet Mistris, for my heart?
You would restore it? No, that's worth a feare,
    As if it were not worthy to be there:
O, keepe it still; for it had rather be
    Your sacrifice, then here remaine with me.
And so I spare it. Come what can become
    Of me, I'le softly tread unto my Tombe;
Or like a Ghost walke silent amongst men,
    Till I may see both it and you agen.

An Elegie

Let me be what I am, as *Virgil* cold;
    As *Horace* fat; or as *Anacreon* old;
No Poets verses yet did ever move,
    Whose Readers did not thinke he was in love.
Who shall forbid me then in Rithme to bee
    As light, and active as the youngest hee
That from the Muses fountaines doth indorse
    His lynes, and hourely sits the Poets horse?
Put on my Ivy Garland, let me see
    Who frownes, who jealous is, who taxeth me.
Fathers, and Husbands, I doe claime a right
    In all that is call'd lovely: take my sight
Sooner then my affection from the faire.
    No face, no hand, proportion, line, or Ayre
Of beautie; but the Muse hath interest in:
    There is not worne that lace, purle, knot or pin,
But is the Poëts matter: And he must,
    When he is furious, love, although not lust.
But then consent, your Daughters and your Wives,
    (If they be faire and worth it) have their lives
Made longer by our praises. Or, if not,
    Wish, you had fowle ones, and deformed got;
Curst in their Cradles, or there chang'd by Elves,
    So to be sure you doe injoy your selves.
Yet keepe those up in sackcloth too, or lether,
    For Silke will draw some sneaking Songster thither.
It is a ryming Age, and Verses swarme
    At every stall; The Cittie Cap's a charme.
But I who live, and have liv'd twentie yeare
    Where I may handle Silke, as free, and neere,
As any Mercer; or the whale-bone man
    That quilts those bodies, I have leave to span:
Have eaten with the Beauties, and the wits,

And braveries of Court, and felt their fits
Of love, and hate: and came so nigh to know
    Whether their faces were their owne, or no:
It is not likely I should now looke downe
    Upon a Velvet Petticote, or a Gowne,
Whose like I have knowne the Taylors Wife put on
    To doe her Husbands rites in, e're 'twere gone
Home to the Customer: his Letcherie
    Being, the best clothes still to praeoccupie.
Put a Coach-mare in Tissue, must I horse
    Her presently? Or leape thy Wife of force,
When by thy sordid bountie she hath on
    A Gowne of that, was the Caparison?
So I might dote upon thy Chaires, and Stooles,
    That are like cloath'd: must I be of those fooles
Of race accompted, that no passion have
    But when thy Wife (as thou conceiv'st) is brave?
Then ope thy wardrobe, thinke me that poore Groome
    That from the Foot-man, when he was become
An Officer there, did make most solemne love,
    To ev'ry Petticote he brush'd, and Glove
He did lay up, and would adore the shooe,
    Or slipper was left off, and kisse it too,
Court every hanging Gowne, and after that,
    Lift up some one, and doe, I tell not what.
Thou didst tell me; and wert o're-joy'd to peepe
    In at a hole, and see these Actions creepe
From the poore wretch, which though he play'd in prose,
    He would have done in verse, with any of those
Wrung on the Withers, by Lord Loves despight,
    Had he'had the facultie to reade, and write!
Such Songsters there are store of; witnesse he
    That chanc'd the lace, laid on a Smock, to see,
And straight-way spent a Sonnet; with that other
    That (in pure Madrigall) unto his Mother
Commended the French-hood, and Scarlet gowne

The Lady Mayresse pass'd in through the Towne,
Unto the Spittle Sermon. O, what strange
   Varietie of Silkes were on th'Exchange!
Or in Moore-fields, this other night! sings one,
   Another answers, 'Lasse, those Silkes are none,
In smiling *L'envoye*, as he would deride
   Any Comparison had with his Cheap-side.
And vouches both the Pageant, and the Day,
   When not the Shops, but windowes doe display
The Stuffes, the Velvets, Plushes, Fringes, Lace,
   And all the originall riots of the place:
Let the poore fooles enjoy their follies, love
   A Goat in Velvet; or some block could move
Under that cover; an old Mid-wives hat!
   Or a Close-stoole so cas'd; or any fat
Bawd, in a Velvet scabberd! I envy
   None of their pleasures! nor will aske thee, why
Thou art jealous of thy Wifes, or Daughters Case:
   More then of eithers manners, wit, or face!

An Execration upon *Vulcan*

And why to me this, thou lame Lord of fire,
  What had I done that might call on thine ire?
Or urge thy Greedie flame, thus to devoure
  So many my Yeares-labours in an houre?
I ne're attempted, *Vulcan*, 'gainst thy life;
  Nor made least line of love to thy loose Wife;
Or in remembrance of thy afront, and scorne,
  With Clownes, and Tradesmen, kept thee clos'd in horne.
'Twas *Jupiter* that hurl'd thee headlong downe,
  And *Mars*, that gave thee a Lanthorne for a Crowne.
Was it because thou wert of old denied
  By *Jove* to have *Minerva* for thy Bride,
That since thou tak'st all envious care and paine,
  To ruine any issue of the braine?
Had I wrote treason there, or heresie,
  Imposture, witchcraft, charmes, or blasphemie,
I had deserv'd, then, thy consuming lookes,
  Perhaps, to have beene burned with my bookes.
But, on thy malice, tell me, didst thou spie
  Any, least loose, or scurrile paper, lie
Conceal'd, or kept there, that was fit to be,
  By thy owne vote, a sacrifice to thee?
Did I there wound the honour of the Crowne?
  Or taxe the Glories of the Church, and Gowne?
Itch to defame the State? or brand the Times?
  And my selfe most, in some selfe-boasting Rimes?
If none of these, then why this fire? Or find
  A cause before; or leave me one behind.
Had I compil'd from *Amadis de Gaule*,
  Th'*Esplandians, Arthurs, Palmerins*, and all
The learned Librarie of *Don Quixote*;
  And so some goodlier monster had begot:

Or spun out Riddles, and weav'd fiftie tomes

    Of *Logogriphes*, and curious *Palindromes*,

Or pomp'd for those hard trifles, *Anagrams*,

    Or *Eteostichs*, or those finer flammes

Of Egges, and Halberds, Cradles, and a Herse,

    A paire of Scisars, and a Combe in verse;

Acrostichs, and *Telestichs*, on jumpe names,

    Thou then hadst had some colour for thy flames,

On such my serious follies; But, thou'lt say,

    There were some pieces of as base allay,

And as false stampe there; parcels of a Play,

    Fitter to see the fire-light, then the day;

Adulterate moneys, such as might not goe:

    Thou should'st have stay'd, till publike fame said so.

Shee is the Judge, Thou Executioner:

    Or if thou needs would'st trench upon her power,

Thou mightst have yet enjoy'd thy crueltie

    With some more thrift, and more varietie:

Thou mightst have had me perish, piece, by piece,

    To light Tobacco, or save roasted Geese,

Sindge Capons, or poore Pigges, dropping their eyes;

    Condemn'd me to the Ovens with the pies;

And so, have kept me dying a whole age,

    Not ravish'd all hence in a minutes rage.

But that's a marke, wherof thy Rites doe boast,

    To make consumption, ever, where thou go'st;

Had I fore-knowne of this thy least desire

    T'have held a Triumph, or a feast of fire,

Especially in paper; that, that steame

    Had tickled your large Nosthrill: many a Reame

To redeeme mine, I had sent in; Enough,

    Thou should'st have cry'd, and all beene proper stuffe.

The *Talmud*, and the *Alcoran* had come,

    With pieces of the *Legend*; The whole summe

Of errant Knight-hood, with their Dames, and Dwarfes,

    Their charmed Boates, and their inchanted Wharfes;

The *Tristrams*, *Lanc'lots*, *Turpins*, and the *Peers*,
   All the madde *Rolands*, and sweet *Oliveers*;
To *Merlins* Marvailes, and his *Caballs* losse,
   With the Chimaera of the *Rosie-Crosse*,
Their Seales, their Characters, Hermetique rings,
   Their Jemme of Riches, and bright Stone, that brings
Invisibilitie, and strength, and tongues:
   The art of kindling the true Coale, by Lungs:
With *Nicholas Pasquill's*, Meddle with your match,
   And the strong lines, that so the time doe catch:
Or Captaine *Pamphlets* horse, and foot, that sallie
   Upon th'Exchange, still, out of Popes-head-Alley;
The weekly Corrants, with *Pauls* Seale; and all
   Th'admir'd discourses of the Prophet *Ball*:
These, had'st thou pleas'd either to dine, or sup,
   Had made a meale for *Vulcan* to lick up.
But in my Deske, what was there to accite
   So ravenous, and vast an appetite?
I dare not say a body, but some parts
   There were of search, and mastry in the Arts.
All the old *Venusine*, in *Poetrie*,
   And lighted by the *Stagirite*, could spie,
Was there made English: with a Grammar too,
   To teach some that, their Nurses could not doe,
The puritie of Language; and among
   The rest, my journey into *Scotland* song,
With all th'adventures; Three bookes not afraid
   To speake the fate of the *Sicilian* Maid
To our owne Ladyes; and in storie there
   Of our fift *Henry*, eight of his nine yeare;
Wherein was oyle, beside the succour spent,
   Which noble *Carew, Cotton, Selden* lent:
And twice-twelve-yeares stor'd up humanitie,
   With humble Gleanings in Divinitie,
After the Fathers, and those wiser Guides
   Whom Faction had not drawne to studie sides.

How in these ruines, *Vulcan*, thou dost lurke,
   All soote, and embers! odious, as thy worke!
I now begin to doubt, if ever Grace,
   Or Goddesse, could be patient of thy face.
Thou woo *Minerva*! or to wit aspire!
   'Cause thou canst halt, with us, in Arts, and Fire!
Sonne of the Wind! for so thy mother gone
   With lust conceiv'd thee; Father thou hadst none:
When thou wert borne, and that thou look'st at best,
   She durst not kisse, but flung thee from her brest.
And so did *Jove*, who ne're meant thee his Cup:
   No mar'le the Clownes of *Lemnos* tooke thee up,
For none but Smiths would have made thee a God.
   Some Alchimist there may be yet, or odde
Squire of the Squibs, against the Pageant day,
   May to thy name a *Vulcanale* say;
And for it lose his eyes with Gun-powder,
   As th'other may his braines with Quicksilver.
Well fare the wise-men yet, on the *Banckside*,
   My friends, the Watermen! They could provide
Against thy furie, when to serve their needs,
   They made a *Vulcan* of a sheafe of Reedes,
Whom they durst handle in their holy-day coates,
   And safely trust to dresse, not burne their Boates.
But, O those Reeds! thy meere disdaine of them,
   Made thee beget that cruell Stratagem,
(Which, some are pleas'd to stile but thy madde pranck)
   Against the *Globe*, the Glory of the *Banke*.
Which, though it were the Fort of the whole Parish,
   Flanck'd with a Ditch, and forc'd out of a Marish,
I saw with two poore Chambers taken in,
   And raz'd, e're thought could urge, This might have bin!
See the worlds Ruines! nothing but the piles
   Left! and wit since to cover it with Tiles.
The Brethren, they streight nois'd it out for Newes,
   'Twas verily some Relique of the Stewes:

And this a Sparkle of that fire let loose
    That was rak'd up in the *Winchestrian* Goose
Bred on the *Banck*, in time of Poperie,
    When *Venus* there maintain'd the Misterie.
But, others fell with that conceipt by the eares,
    And cry'd, it was a threatning to the beares;
And that accursed ground, the *Parish-Garden*:
    Nay, sigh'd a Sister, 'twas the Nun, *Kate Arden*,
Kindled the fire! But then, did one returne,
    No Foole would his owne harvest spoile, or burne!
If that were so, thou rather would'st advance
    The place, that was thy Wives inheritance.
O no, cry'd all, *Fortune*, for being a whore,
    Scap'd not his Justice any jot the more:
He burnt that Idoll of the *Revels* too:
    Nay, let *White-Hall* with Revels have to doe,
Though but in daunces, it shall know his power;
    There was a Judgement shew'n too in an houre.
Hee is true *Vulcan* still! He did not spare
    Troy, though it were so much his *Venus* care.
Foole, wilt thou let that in example come?
    Did not she save from thence, to build a *Rome*?
And what hast thou done in these pettie spights,
    More then advanc'd the houses, and their rites?
I will not argue thee, from those, of guilt,
    For they were burnt, but to be better built.
'Tis true, that in thy wish they were destroy'd,
    Which thou hast only vented, not enjoy'd.
So would'st thou have run upon the *Rolls* by stealth,
    And didst invade part of the Common-wealth,
In those Records, which, were all Chroniclers gone,
    Will be remembered by *Six Clerkes*, to one.
But say, all sixe good men, what answer yee?
    Lyes there no Writ out of the *Chancerie*,
Against this *Vulcan*? No Injunction?
    No order? no Decree? Though we be gone

At *Common-Law*: me thinkes in his despight
  A Court of *Equitie* should doe us right,
But to confine him to the Brew-houses,
  The Glasse-house, Dye-fats, and their Fornaces;
To live in Sea-coale, and goe forth in smoake;
  Or lest that vapour might the Citie choake,
Condemne him to the Brick-kills, or some Hill-foot (out in
  Sussex) to an iron Mill;
Or in small Fagots have him blaze about
  Vile Tavernes, and the Drunkards pisse him out;
Or in the *Bell*-Mans Lanthorne, like a spie,
  Burne to a snuffe, and then stinke out, and die:
I could invent a sentence, yet were worse;
  But I'le conclude all in a civil curse.
Pox on your flameship, *Vulcan*; if it be
  To all as fatall as 't hath beene to me,
And to *Pauls-Steeple*; which was unto us
  'Bove all your Fire-workes, had at *Ephesus*,
Or *Alexandria*; and though a Divine
  Losse, remaines yet, as unrepair'd as mine.
Would you had kept your Forge, at *Aetna* still,
  And there made Swords, Bills, Glaves, and Armes your fill;
Maintain'd the trade at *Bilbo*, or else-where;
  Strooke in at *Millan* with the Cutlers there;
Or stay'd but where the Fryar, and you first met,
  Who from the Divels-Arse did Guns beget;
Or fixt in the *Low-Countrey's*, where you might
  On both sides doe your mischiefes with delight;
Blow up, and ruine, myne, and countermyne,
  Make your Petards, and Granats, all your fine
Engines of Murder, and receive the praise
  Of massacring Man-kind so many wayes.
We aske your absence here, we all love peace,
  And pray the fruites thereof, and the increase;
So doth the *King*, and most of the *Kings men*
  That have good places: therefore once agen,

Pox on thee, *Vulcan*, thy *Pandora's* pox,
    And all the Evils that flew out of her box
Light on thee: Or if those plagues will not doo,
    Thy Wives pox on thee, and *Bess Broughtons* too.

An Epistle answering to one that asked to be Sealed of the Tribe of Ben

Men that are safe, and sure, in all they doe,
    Care not what trials they are put unto;
They meet the fire, the Test, as Martyrs would;
    And though Opinion stampe them not, are gold.
I could say more of such, but that I flie
    To speake my selfe out too ambitiously,
And shewing so weake an Act to vulgar eyes,
    Put conscience and my right to compromise.
Let those that meerely talke, and never thinke,
    That live in the wild Anarchie of Drinke,
Subject to quarrell only; or else such
    As make it their proficiencie, how much
They'have glutted in, and letcher'd out that weeke,
    That never yet did friend, or friendship seeke
But for a Sealing: let these men protest.
    Or th'other on their borders, that will jeast
On all Soules that are absent; even the dead;
    Like flies, or wormes, which mans corrupt parts fed:
That to speake well, thinke it above all sinne,
    Of any Companie but that they are in,
Call every night to Supper in these fitts,
    And are received for the Covey of Witts;
That censure all the Towne, and all th'affaires,
    And know whose ignorance is more then theirs;
Let these men have their wayes, and take their times
    To vent their Libels, and to issue rimes,
I have no portion in them, nor their deale
    Of newes they get, to strew out the long meale,
I studie other friendships, and more one,
    Then these can ever be; or else wish none.
What is't to me whether the French Designe
    Be, or be not, to get the *Val-telline*?

Or the States Ships sent forth belike to meet
    Some hopes of *Spaine* in their West-Indian Fleet?
Whether the Dispensation yet be sent,
    Or that the Match from *Spaine* was ever meant?
I wish all well, and pray high heaven conspire
    My Princes safetie, and my Kings desire,
But if, for honour, we must draw the Sword,
    And force back that, which will not be restor'd,
I have a body, yet, that spirit drawes
    To live, or fall a Carkasse in the cause.
So farre without inquirie what the States,
    Brunsfield, and *Mansfield* doe this yeare, my fates
Shall carry me at Call; and I'le be well,
    Though I doe neither heare these newes, nor tell
Of *Spaine* or *France*; or were not prick'd downe one
    Of the late Mysterie of reception,
Although my Fame, to his, not under-heares,
    That guides the Motions, and directs the beares.
But that's a blow, by which in time I may
    Lose all my credit with my Christmas Clay,
And animated *Porc'lane* of the Court,
    I, and for this neglect, the courser sort
Of earthen Jarres, there may molest me too:
    Well, with mine owne fraile Pitcher, what to doe
I have decreed; keepe it from waves, and presse;
    Lest it be justled, crack'd, made nought, or lesse:
Live to that point I will, for which I am man,
    And dwell as in my Center, as I can,
Still looking to, and ever loving heaven;
    With reverence using all the gifts thence given.
'Mongst which, if I have any friendships sent,
    Such as are square, wel-tagde, and permanent,
Not built with Canvasse, paper, and false lights,
    As are the Glorious Scenes, at the great sights;
And that there be no fev'ry heats, nor colds,
    Oylie Expansions, or shrunke durtie folds,

But all so cleare, and led by reasons flame,
    As but to stumble in her sight were shame;
These I will honour, love, embrace, and serve:
    And free it from all question to preserve.
So short you read my Character, and theirs
    I would call mine, to which not many Staires
Are asked to climbe. First give me faith, who know
    My selfe a little. I will take you so,
As you have writ your selfe. Now stand, and then,
    Sir, you are Sealed of the Tribe of *Ben*.

To the immortall memorie, and friendship of that
noble paire, Sir Lucius Cary, and Sir H. Morison

The Turne

Brave Infant of *Saguntum*, cleare
Thy comming forth in that great yeare,
When the Prodigious *Hannibal* did crowne
His rage, with razing your immortall Towne.
Thou, looking then about,
E're thou wert halfe got out,
Wise child, did'st hastily returne,
And mad'st thy Mothers wombe thine urne.
How summ'd a circle didst thou leave man-kind
Of deepest lore, could we the Center find!

The Counter-turne

Did wiser Nature draw thee back,
From out the horrour of that sack?
Where shame, faith, honour, and regard of right
Lay trampled on; the deeds of death, and night,
Urg'd, hurried forth, and horld
Upon th'affrighted world:
Sword, fire, and famine, with fell fury met;
And all on utmost ruine set;
As, could they but lifes miseries fore-see,
No doubt all Infants would returne like thee.

The Stand

For, what is life, if measur'd by the space,
Not by the act?
Or masked man, if valu'd by his face,
Above his fact?
Here's one out-liv'd his Peeres,

And told forth fourescore yeares;
He vexed time, and busied the whole State;
Troubled both foes, and friends;
But ever to no ends:
What did this Stirrer, but die late?
How well at twentie had he falne, or stood!
For three of his foure-score, he did no good.

THE TURNE

Hee entred well, by vertuous parts,
Got up and thriv'd with honest arts:
He purchas'd friends, and fame, and honours then,
And had his noble name advanc'd with men:
But weary of that flight,
Hee stoop'd in all mens sight
To sordid flatteries, acts of strife,
And sunke in that dead sea of life
So deep, as he did then death's waters sup;
But that the Corke of Title boy'd him up.

THE COUNTER-TURNE

Alas, but *Morison* fell young:
Hee never fell, thou fall'st, my tongue.
Hee stood, a Souldier to the last right end,
A perfect Patriot, and a noble friend,
But most, a vertuous Sonne.
All Offices were done
By him, so ample, full, and round,
In weight, in measure, number, sound,
As though his age imperfect might appeare,
His life was of Humanitie the Spheare.

THE STAND

Goe now, and tell out dayes summ'd up with feares,
And make them yeares;

Produce thy masse of miseries on the Stage,
To swell thine age;
Repeat of things a throng,
To shew thou hast beene long,
Not liv'd; for Life doth her great actions spell,
By what was done and wrought
In season, and so brought
To light: her measures are, how well
Each syllab'e answer'd, and was form'd, how faire;
These make the lines of life, and that's her ayre.

The Turne

It is not growing like a tree
In bulke, doth make man better bee;
Or standing long an Oake, three hundred yeare,
To fall a logge at last, dry, bald, and seare:
A Lillie of a Day,
Is fairer farre, in May,
Although it fall, and die that night;
It was the Plant, and flowre of light.
In small proportions, we just beautie see:
And in short measures, life may perfect bee.

The Counter-turne

Call, noble *Lucius*, then for Wine,
And let thy lookes with gladnesse shine:
Accept this garland, plant it on thy head,
And thinke, nay know, thy *Morison's* not dead.
Hee leap'd the present age,
Possest with holy rage,
To see that bright eternall Day:
Of which we *Priests*, and *Poëts* say
Such truths, as we expect for happy men,
And there he lives with memorie; and *Ben*

The Stand

Jonson, who sung this of him, e're he went
Himselfe to rest,
Or taste a part of that full joy he meant
To have exprest,
In this bright *Asterisme*:
Where it were friendships schisme,
(Were not his *Lucius* long with us to tarry)
To separate these twi-
Lights, the *Dioscuri*;
And keepe the one halfe from his *Harry*.
But fate doth so alternate the designe,
Whilst that in heav'n, this light on earth must shine.

The Turne

And shine as you exalted are;
Two names of friendship, but one Starre:
Of hearts the union. And those not by chance
Made, or indentur'd, or leas'd out t'advance
The profits for a time.
No pleasures vaine did chime,
Of rimes, or ryots, at your feasts,
Orgies of drinke, or fain'd protests:
But simple love of greatnesse, and of good;
That knits brave minds, and manners, more then blood.

The Counter-turne

This made you first to know the Why
You lik'd, then after, to apply
That liking; and approach so one the tother,
Till either grew a portion of the other:
Each stiled, by his end,
The Copie of his friend.
You liv'd to be the great surnames,

And titles, by which all made claimes
Unto the Vertue. Nothing perfect done,
But as a CARY, or a MORISON.

THE STAND

And such a force the faire example had,
As they that saw
The good, and durst not practise it, were glad
That such a Law
Was left yet to Man-kind;
Where they might read, and find
Friendship, in deed, was written, not in words:
And with the heart, not pen,
Of two so early men,
Whose lines her rowles were, and records.
Who, e're the first downe bloomed on the chin,
Had sow'd these fruits, and got the harvest in.

The humble Petition of poore *Ben*. To th'best of Monarchs, Masters, Men, King Charles

. . . Doth most humbly show it,
To your Majestie your Poët:

That whereas your royall *Father*,
JAMES *the blessed*, pleas'd the rather,
Of his speciall grace to *Letters*,
To make all the MUSES debters
To his bountie; by extension
Of a free Poëtique Pension,
A large hundred Markes annuitie,
To be given me in gratuitie
For done service, and to come:
   And that this so accepted summe,
Or dispenc'd in bookes, or bread,
(For with both the MUSE was fed)
Hath drawne on me, from the times,
All the envie of the *Rymes*,
And the ratling pit-pat-noyse,
Of the lesse-*Poëtique* boyes;
When their pot-guns ayme to hit,
With their pellets of small wit,
Parts of me (they judg'd) decay'd,
But we last out, still unlay'd.
   Please your Majestie to make
Of your grace, for goodnesse sake,
Those your *Fathers Markes*, your *Pounds*;
Let their spite (which now abounds)
Then goe on, and doe its worst;
This would all their envie burst:
And so warme the *Poëts* tongue
You'ld reade a Snake, in his next Song.

An Elegie on the Lady *Jane Pawlet*, Marchion: of *Winton*

What gentle Ghost, besprent with *April* deaw,
    Hayles me, so solemnly, to yonder Yewgh?
And beckning wooes me, from the fatall tree
    To pluck a Garland, for her selfe, or mee?
I doe obey you, Beautie! for in death,
    You seeme a faire one! O that you had breath,
To give your shade a name! Stay, stay, I feele
    A horrour in mee! all my blood is steele!
Stiffe! starke! my joynts 'gainst one another knock!
    Whose Daughter? ha? Great *Savage* of the Rock?
Hee's good, as great. I am almost a stone!
    And e're I can aske more of her, shee's gone!
Alas, I am all Marble! write the rest
    Thou wouldst have written, Fame, upon my brest:
It is a large faire table, and a true,
    And the disposure will be something new,
When I, who would her Poët have become,
    At least may beare th'inscription to her Tombe.
Shee was the Lady *Jane*, and *Marchionisse*
    Of *Winchester*; the Heralds can tell this:
Earle *Rivers* Grand-Child – serve not formes, good Fame,
    Sound thou her Vertues, give her soule a Name.
Had I a thousand Mouthes, as many Tongues,
    And voyce to raise them from my brazen Lungs,
I durst not aime at that: The dotes were such
    Thereof, no notion can expresse how much
Their Carract was! I, or my trump must breake,
    But rather I, should I of that part speake!
It is too neere of kin to Heaven, the Soule,
    To be describ'd! Fames fingers are too foule
To touch these Mysteries! We may admire
    The blaze, and splendor, but not handle fire!

What she did here, by great example, well,
    T'inlive posteritie, her Fame may tell!
And, calling truth to witnesse, make that good
    From the inherent Graces in her blood!
Else, who doth praise a person by a new,
    But a fain'd way, doth rob it of the true.
Her Sweetnesse, Softnesse, her faire Courtesie,
    Her wary guardes, her wise simplicitie,
Were like a ring of Vertues, 'bout her set,
    And pietie the Center, where all met,
A reverend State she had, an awfull Eye,
    A dazling, yet inviting, Majestie:
What Nature, Fortune, Institution, Fact
    Could summe to a perfection, was her Act!
How did she leave the world? with what contempt?
    Just as she in it liv'd! and so exempt
From all affection! when they urg'd the Cure
    Of her disease, how did her soule assure
Her suffrings, as the body had beene away!
    And to the Torturers (her Doctors) say,
Stick on your Cupping-glasses, feare not, put
    Your hottest Causticks to, burne, lance, or cut:
'Tis but a body which you can torment,
    And I, into the world, all Soule, was sent!
Then comforted her Lord! and blest her Sonne!
    Chear'd her faire Sisters in her race to runne!
With gladnesse temper'd her sad Parents teares!
    Made her friends joyes to get above their feares!
And, in her last act, taught the Standers-by,
    With admiration, and applause to die!
Let Angels sing her glories, who did call
    Her spirit home, to her originall!
Who saw the way was made it! and were sent
    To carry, and conduct the Complement
'Twixt death and life! Where her mortalitie
    Became her Birth-day to Eternitie!

142

And now, through circumfused light, she lookes
    On Natures secrets, there, as her owne bookes:
Speakes Heavens Language! and discourseth free
    To every *Order*, ev'ry *Hierarchie*!
Beholds her Maker! and, in him, doth see
    What the beginnings of all beauties be;
And all beatitudes, that thence doe flow:
    Which they that have the Crowne are sure to know!
Goe now, her happy Parents, and be sad,
    If you not understand, what Child you had.
If you dare grudge at Heaven, and repent
    T'have paid againe a blessing was but lent,
And trusted so, as it deposited lay
    At pleasure, to be call'd for, every day!
If you can envie your owne Daughters blisse,
    And wish her state lesse happie then it is!
If you can cast about your either eye,
    And see all dead here, or about to dye!
The Starres, that are the Jewels of the Night,
    And Day, deceasing with the Prince of light,
The Sunne! great Kings, and mightiest Kingdomes fall!
    Whole Nations! nay, Mankind! the World, with all
That ever had beginning there, to have end!
    With what injustice should one soule pretend
T'escape this common knowne necessitie,
    When we were all borne, we began to die;
And, but for that Contention, and brave strife
    The Christian hath t'enjoy the future life,
Hee were the wretched'st of the race of men:
    But as he soares at that, he bruiseth then
The Serpents head: Gets above Death, and Sinne,
    And, sure of Heaven, rides triumphing in.

Eupheme;
Or, The Faire Fame Left to Posteritie

Of that truly-noble Lady, the Lady VENETIA DIGBY,
late Wife of Sir KENELME DIGBY, Knight:
A Gentleman absolute in all Numbers;

Consisting of these Ten Pieces

> *The Dedication of her CRADLE*
> *The Song of her DESCENT*
> *The Picture of her BODY*
> *Her MIND*
> *Her being chosen a MUSE*
> *Her faire OFFICES*
> *Her happie MATCH*
> *Her hopefull ISSUE*
> *Her APOTHEOSIS, or Relation to the Saints*
> *Her Inscription, or CROWNE*

Vivam amare voluptas, defunctam Religios

STATIUS

1. THE DEDICATION OF HER CRADLE

Faire FAME, who art ordain'd to crowne
With ever-greene, and great renowne,
Their Heads, that ENVY would hold downe
       With her, in shade

Of Death, and Darknesse; and deprive
Their names of being kept alive,
By THEE, and CONSCIENCE, both who thrive
       By the just trade

Of Goodnesse still: Vouchsafe to take
This CRADLE, and for Goodnesse sake,
A dedicated Ensigne make
        Thereof, to TIME.

That all Posteritie, as wee,
Who read what the CREPUNDIA bee,
May something by that twilight see
        'Bove rattling Rime.

For, though that Rattles, Timbrels, Toyes,
Take little Infants with their noyse,
As prop'rest gifts, to Girles, and Boyes,
        Of light expence;

Their Corrals, Whistles, and prime Coates,
Their painted Maskes, their paper Boates,
With Sayles of silke, as the first notes
        Surprize their sense:

Yet, here are no such Trifles brought,
No cobweb Call's; no Surcoates wrought
With Gold, or Claspes, which might be bought
        On every Stall.

But, here's a Song of her DESCENT;
And Call to the high Parliament
Of Heaven; where SERAPHIM take tent
        Of ord'ring all.

This, utter'd by an antient BARD,
Who claimes (of reverence) to be heard,
As comming with his Harpe, prepar'd
        To chant her 'gree,

Is sung: as also her getting up
By JACOBS Ladder, to the top
Of that eternall Port kept ope'
        For such as SHEE.

2. The Song of her descent

I sing the just, and uncontrol'd Descent
    Of Dame VENETIA DIGBY, styl'd The Faire:
For Mind, and Body, the most excellent
    That ever Nature, or the later Ayre
Gave two such Houses as NORTHUMBERLAND,
    And STANLEY, to the which shee was Co-heire.
Speake it, you bold PENATES, you that stand
    At either Stemme, and know the veines of good
Run from your rootes; Tell, testifie the grand
    Meeting of Graces, that so swell'd the flood
Of vertues in her, as, in short, shee grew
    The wonder of her Sexe, and of your Blood.
And tell thou, ALDE-LEGH, None can tell more true
    Thy Neeces line, then thou that gav'st thy Name
Into the Kindred, whence thy *Adam* drew
    Meschines honour with the *Cestrian* fame
Of the first *Lupus*, to the Familie
    By *Ranulph* . . .

[The rest of this Song is lost.]

3. The Picture of the Body

Sitting, and ready to be drawne,
    What make these Velvets, Silkes, and Lawne,
    Embroderies, Feathers, Fringes, Lace
    Where every lim takes like a face?
Send these suspected helpes, to aide
    Some Forme defective, or decay'd;
    This beautie without falshood fayre,
    Needs nought to cloath it but the ayre.

Yet something, to the Painters view,
    Were fitly interpos'd; so new:
    Hee shall, if he can understand,
    Worke with my fancie, his owne hand.

Draw first a Cloud: all save her neck;
     And, out of that, make Day to breake;
     Till, like her face, it doe appeare,
     And Men may thinke, all light rose there.

Then let the beames of that, disperse
     The Cloud, and show the Universe;
     But at such distance, as the eye
     May rather yet adore, then spy.

The Heaven design'd, draw next a Spring,
     With all that Youth, or it can bring:
     Foure Rivers branching forth like Seas,
     And Paradise confining these.

Last, draw the circles of this Globe,
     And let there be a starry Robe
     Of Constellations 'bout her horld;
     And thou hast painted beauties world.

But, Painter, see thou doe not sell
     A copie of this peece; nor tell
     Whose 'tis: but if it favour find
     Next sitting we will draw her mind.

4. THE MIND

Painter, yo'are come, but may be gone,
     Now I have better thought thereon,
     This worke I can performe alone;
     And give you reasons more then one.

Not, that your Art I doe refuse:
     But here I may no colours use.
     Beside, your hand will never hit,
     To draw a thing that cannot sit.

You could make shift to paint an Eye,
     An Eagle towring in the sky,

The Sunne, a Sea, or soundlesse Pit;
    But these are like a Mind, not it.

No, to expresse a Mind to sense,
    Would aske a Heavens Intelligence;
    Since nothing can report that flame,
    But what's of kinne to whence it came.

Sweet Mind, then speake your selfe, and say,
    As you goe on, by what brave way
    Our sense you doe with knowledge fill,
    And yet remaine our wonder still.

I call you *Muse*; now make it true:
    Hence-forth may every line be you;
    That all may say, that see the frame,
    This is no Picture, but the same.

A mind so pure, so perfect fine,
    As 'tis not radiant, but divine:
    And so disdaining any tryer;
'Tis got where it can try the fire.

    There, high exalted in the Spheare,
    As it another Nature were,
    It moveth all; and makes a flight
    As circular, as infinite.

Whose Notions when it will expresse
    In speech; it is with that excesse
    Of grace, and Musique to the eare,
    As what it spoke, it planted there.

The Voyce so sweet, the words so faire,
    As some soft chime had stroak'd the ayre;
    And, though the sound were parted thence,
    Still left an Eccho in the sense.

But, that a Mind so rapt, so high,
    So swift, so pure, should yet apply

It selfe to us, and come so nigh
Earths grossnesse; There's the how, and why.

Is it because it sees us dull,
  And stuck in clay here, it would pull
  Us forth, by some Celestiall slight
  Up to her owne sublimed hight?

Or hath she here, upon the ground,
  Some Paradise, or Palace found
  In all the bounds of beautie fit
  For her t'inhabit? There is it.

Thrice happy house, that hast receipt
  For this so loftie forme, so streight,
  So polisht, perfect, round, and even,
  As it slid moulded off from Heaven.

  Not swelling like the Ocean proud,
  But stooping gently, as a Cloud,
  As smooth as Oyle pour'd forth, and calme
  As showers; and sweet as drops of Balme.

Smooth, soft, and sweet, in all a floud
  Where it may run to any good;
  And where it stayes, it there becomes
  A nest of odorous spice, and gummes.

In action, winged as the wind,
  In rest, like spirits left behind
  Upon a banke, or field of flowers,
  Begotten by that wind, and showers.

In thee, faire Mansion, let it rest,
  Yet know, with what thou art possest,
  Thou entertaining in thy brest,
  But such a Mind, mak'st God thy Guest.

8.

A whole quaternion in the middest of this Poem is lost, containing entirely the three next pieces of it, and all of the fourth (which in the order of the whole, is the eighth) excepting the very end: which at the top of the next quaternion goeth on thus:

But, for you (growing Gentlemen) the happy branches of two so illustrious Houses as these, wherefrom your honour'd Mother is in both lines descended; let me leave you this last Legacie of Counsell; which so soone as you arrive at yeares of mature Understanding, open you (Sir) that are the eldest, and read it to your Brethren, for it will concerne you all alike. Vowed by a faithfull Servant, and Client of your Familie, with his latest breath expiring it,

B.J.

To Kenelme, John, George

Boast not these Titles of your Ancestors;
   (Brave Youths) they'are their possessions, none of yours:
When your owne Vertues, equall'd have their Names,
   'Twill be but faire, to leane upon their *Fames*;
For they are strong Supporters: But, till then,
   The greatest are but growing Gentlemen.
It is a wretched thing to trust to reedes;
   Which all men doe, that urge not their owne deeds
Up to their Ancestors; the rivers side,
   By which yo'are planted, shew's your fruit shall bide.
Hang all your roomes, with one large Pedigree:
   'Tis Vertue alone, is true Nobilitie.
Which Vertue from your Father, ripe, will fall;
   Study illustrious Him, and you have all.

9. ELEGIE ON MY MUSE

The truly honoured Lady, the Lady VENETIA DIGBY;
who living, gave me leave to call her so.
                              Being
    Her APOTHEOSIS, *or Relation to the Saints.*

Sera quidem tanto struitur medicina dolori

'Twere time that I dy'd too, now shee is dead,
   Who was my *Muse*, and life of all I sey'd,
The Spirit that I wrote with, and conceiv'd;
   All that was good, or great in me she weav'd,
And set it forth; the rest were Cobwebs fine,
   Spun out in name of some of the old *Nine*!
To hang a window, or make darke the roome,
   Till swept away, they were cancell'd with a broome!
Nothing, that could remaine, or yet can stirre
   A sorrow in me, fit to wait to her!
O! had I seene her laid out a faire Corse,
   By *Death*, on Earth, I should have had remorse
On *Nature*, for her: who did let her lie,
   And saw that portion of her selfe to die.
Sleepie, or stupid Nature, couldst thou part
   With such a *Raritie*, and not rowse *Art*
With all her aydes, to save her from the seize
   Of *Vulture death*, and those relentlesse cleies?
Thou wouldst have lost the *Phoenix*, had the kind
   Beene trusted to thee: not to't selfe assign'd.
Looke on thy sloth, and give thy selfe undone,
   (For so thou art with me) now shee is gone.
My wounded mind cannot sustaine this stroke,
   It rages, runs, flies, stands, and would provoke
The world to ruine with it; in her *Fall*,
   I summe up mine owne breaking, and wish all.
Thou hast no more blowes, *Fate*, to drive at one:
   What's left a *Poêt*, when his *Muse* is gone?

Sure, I am dead, and know it not! I feele
   Nothing I doe; but, like a heavie wheele,
Am turned with an others powers. My Passion
   Whoorles me about, and to blaspheme in fashion!
I murmure against *God*, for having ta'en
   Her blessed Soule, hence, forth this valley vane
Of teares, and dungeon of calamitie!
   I envie it the Angels amitie!
The joy of Saints! the *Crowne* for which it lives,
   The glorie, and gaine of rest, which the place gives!
Dare I prophane, so irreligious bee
   To 'greet, or grieve her soft Euthanasee?
So sweetly taken to the Court of blisse,
   As spirits had stolne her *Spirit*, in a kisse,
From off her pillow, and deluded bed;
   And left her lovely body unthought dead!
Indeed, she is not dead! but laid to sleepe
   In earth, till the last *Trumpe* awake the *Sheepe*
And *Goates* together, whither they must come
   To heare their Judge, and his eternall doome;
To have that finall retribution,
   Expected with the fleshes restitution.
For, as there are three *Natures, Schoolemen* call
   One *corporall*, only; th'other *spirituall*,
Like single; so, there is a third, commixt,
   Of *Body* and *Spirit* together, plac'd betwixt
Those other two; which must be judg'd, or crown'd:
   This as it guilty is, or guiltlesse found,
Must come to take a sentence, by the sense
   Of that great Evidence, the *Conscience*!
Who will be there, against that day prepar'd,
   T'accuse, or quit all *Parties* to be heard!
O *Day* of joy, and suretie to the just!
   Who in that feast of *Resurrection* trust!
That great eternall *Holy-day* of rest,
   To Body, and Soule! where *Love* is all the guest!

And the whole *Banquet* is full sight of *God*!
    Of joy the *Circle*, and sole *Period*!
All other gladnesse, with the thought is barr'd;
    Hope, hath her end! and *Faith* hath her reward!
This being thus: why should my tongue, or pen
    Presume to interpell that fulnesse, when
Nothing can more adorne it, then the seat
    That she is in, or, make it more compleat?
Better be dumbe, then superstitious!
    Who violates the God-head, is most vitious
Against the Nature he would worship. *Hee*
    Will honour'd be in all simplicitie!
Have all his actions wondred at, and view'd
    With silence, and amazement! not with rude,
Dull, and prophane, weake, and imperfect eyes,
    Have busie search made in his mysteries!
Hee knowes, what worke h'hath done, to call this *Guest*,
    Out of her noble body, to this *Feast*:
And give her place, according to her blood,
    Amongst her *Peeres*, those Princes of all good!
Saints, *Martyrs*, *Prophets*, with those *Hierarchies*,
    Angels, *Arch-angels*, *Principalities*,
The *Dominations*, *Vertues*, and the *Powers*,
    The *Thrones*, the *Cherube*, and *Seraphick* bowers,
That, planted round, there sing before the *Lamb*,
    A new Song to his praise, and great *I AM*:
And she doth know, out of the shade of Death,
    What 'tis t'enjoy an everlasting breath!
To have her captiv'd spirit freed from flesh,
    And on her Innocence, a garment fresh
And white, as that, put on: and in her hand,
    With boughs of Palme, a crowned *Victrice* stand!
And will you, worthy Sonne, Sir, knowing this,
    Put black, and mourning on? and say you misse
A *Wife*, a *Friend*, a *Lady*, or a *Love*;
    Whom her *Redeemer*, honour'd hath above

Her fellowes, with the oyle of gladnesse, bright
  In Heav'ns *Empyrean*, with a robe of light?
Thither, you hope to come; and there to find
  That pure, that pretious, and exalted mind
You once enjoy'd: A short space severs yee,
  Compar'd unto that long eternitie,
That shall re-joyne yee. Was she, then, so deare,
  When shee departed? you will meet her there,
Much more desir'd, and deárer then before,
  By all the wealth of blessings, and the store
Accumulated on her, by the *Lord*
  Of life, and light, the Sonne of *God*, the *Word*!
There, all the happy soules, that ever were,
  Shall meet with gladnesse in one *Theatre*;
And each shall know, there, one anothers face,
  By beatifick vertue of the Place.
There shall the Brother, with the Sister walke,
  And Sons, and Daughters, with their Parents talke;
But all of *God*; They still shall have to say,
  But make him *All in All*, their *Theme*, that *Day*:
That happy *Day*, that never shall see night!
  Where *Hee* will be, all Beautie to the *Sight*;
Wine, or delicious fruits, unto the *Taste*;
  A Musique in the *Eares*, will ever last;
Unto the *Sent*, a Spicerie, or Balme;
  And to the *Touch*, a Flower, like soft as Palme.
Hee will all Glory, all Perfection be,
  God, in the *Union*, and the *Trinitie*!
That holy, great, and glorious Mysterie,
  Will there revealed be in Majestie!
By light, and comfort of spirituall *Grace*,
  The vision of our *Saviour*, face to face,
In his humanitie! To heare him preach
  The price of our *Redemption*, and to teach
Through his inherent righteousnesse, in death,
  The safetie of our soules, and forfeit breath!

What fulnesse of beatitude is here?
    What love with mercy mixed doth appeare?
To style us Friends, who were, by Nature, Foes?
    Adopt us Heires, by grace, who were of those
Had lost our selves? and prodigally spent
    Our native portions, and possessed rent;
Yet have all debts forgiven us, and advance
    By imputed right to an inheritance
In his eternall Kingdome, where we sit
    Equall with Angels, and Co-heires of it?
Nor dare we under blasphemy conceive
    He that shall be our supreme Judge, should leave
Himselfe so un-inform'd of his elect,
    Who knowes the hearts of all, and can dissect
The smallest Fibre of our flesh; he can
    Find all our Atomes from a point t'a span!
Our closest Creekes, and Corners, and can trace
    Each line, as it were graphick, in the face!
And best he knew her noble Character,
    For 'twas himselfe who form'd, and gave it her.
And to that forme, lent two such veines of blood
    As nature could not more increase the flood
Of title in her! All Nobilitie
    (But pride, that schisme of incivilitie)
She had, and it became her! she was fit
    T'have knowne no envy, but by suffring it!
She had a mind as calme, as she was faire;
    Not tost or troubled with light Lady-aire;
But, kept an even gate, as some streight tree
    Mov'd by the wind, so comely moved she.
And by the awfull manage of her Eye
    She swaid all bus'nesse in the Familie!
To one she said, Doe this, he did it; So
    To another, Move; he went; To a third, Go,
He run; and all did strive with diligence
    T'obey, and serve her sweet Commandements.

She was, in one, a many parts of life;
  A tender *Mother*, a discreeter *Wife*,
A solemne *Mistresse*, and so good a *Friend*,
  So charitable, to religious end,
In all her petite actions, so devote,
  As her whole life was now become one note
Of Pietie, and private holinesse.
  She spent more time in teares her selfe to dresse
For her devotions, and those sad essayes
  Of sorrow, then all pompe of gaudy daies:
And came forth ever cheered, with the rod
  Of divine Comfort, when sh'had talk'd with *God*.
Her broken sighes did never misse whole sense:
  Nor can the bruised heart want eloquence:
For, Prayer is the Incense most perfumes
  The holy Altars, when it least presumes.
And hers were all Humilitie! they beat
  The doore of *Grace*, and found the *Mercy-Seat*.
In frequent speaking by the pious Psalmes
  Her solemne houres she spent, or giving Almes,
Or doing other deeds of Charitie,
  To cloath the naked, feed the hungry. Shee
Would sit in an Infirmery, whole dayes
  Poring, as on a Map, to find the wayes
To that eternall Rest, where now sh'hath place
  By sure Election, and predestin'd grace!
Shee saw her Saviour, by an early light,
  Incarnate in the Manger, shining bright
On all the world! She saw him on the Crosse
  Suffring, and dying to redeeme our losse!
Shee saw him rise, triumphing over Death
  To justifie, and quicken us in breath!
Shee saw him too, in glory to ascend
  For his designed worke, the perfect end
Of raising, judging, and rewarding all
  The kind of Man, on whom his doome should fall!

All this by *Faith* she saw, and fram'd a Plea,
    In manner of a daily *Apostrophe*,
To him should be her Judge, true *God*, true *Man*,
    Jesus, the onely-gotten *Christ*! who can
(As being Redeemer, and Repairer too
    Of lapsed Nature) best know what to doe,
In that great Act of judgement: which the *Father*
    Hath given wholly to the Sonne (the rather
As being the Sonne of *Man*) to shew his *Power*,
    His *Wisdome*, and his *Justice*, in that houre,
The last of houres, and shutter up of all;
    Where first his *Power* will appeare, by call
Of all are dead to life! His *Wisdome* show
    In the discerning of each conscience, so!
And most his *Justice*, in the fitting parts,
    And giving dues to all Mankinds deserts!
In this sweet *Extasie*, she was rapt hence.
    Who reades, will pardon my Intelligence.
That thus have ventur'd these true straines upon;
    To publish her a *Saint*. My *Muse* is gone.

        In pietatis memoriam
          quam praestas
      Venetiae *tuae illustrissim*:
        Marit: *dign*: Digbeie
  Hanc ΑΠΟΘΕΩΣΙΝ, *tibi, tuisque sacro.*

The Tenth, being her Inscription, or CROWNE, is lost.

A Fragment of Petronius Arbiter

Doing, a filthy pleasure is, and short;
And done, we straight repent us of the sport:
Let us not then rush blindly on unto it,
Like lustfull beasts, that onely know to doe it:
For lust will languish, and that heat decay.
But thus, thus, keeping endlesse Holy-day,
Let us together closely lie, and kisse,
There is no labour, nor no shame in this;
This hath pleas'd, doth please, and long will please; never
Can this decay, but is beginning ever.

OTHER POEMS

Ode. *Allegorike*

Who saith our Times nor have, nor can
   Produce us a blacke Swan?
   Behold, where one doth swim;
      Whose Note, and Hue,
Besides the other Swannes admiring him,
   Betray it true:
   A gentler Bird, then this,
Did never dint the breast of *Tamisis.*

Marke, marke, but when his wing he takes,
   How faire a flight he makes!
   How upward, and direct!
      Whil'st pleas'd *Apollo*
Smiles in his Sphaere, to see the rest affect,
      In vaine to follow:
   This Swanne is onely his,
And *Phoebus* love cause of his blackenesse is.

He shew'd him first the hoofe-cleft Spring,
   Neere which, the *Thespiad's* sing;
   The cleare *Dircaen* Fount
      Where *Pindar* swamme;
The pale *Pyrene*, and the forked *Mount*:
      And, when they came
   To brookes, and broader streames,
From *Zephyr's* rape would close him with his beames.

This change'd his Downe; till this, as white
   As the whole heard in sight,
   And still is in the Brest:
      That part nor Winde,
Nor Sunne could make to vary from the rest,
      Or alter kinde.
   So much doth Virtue hate,
For stile of rarenesse, to degenerate.

Be then both Rare, and Good; and long
    Continue thy sweete Song.
        Nor let one River boast
        Thy tunes alone;
But prove the Aire, and saile from Coast to Coast:
    Salute old *Mône*,
    But first to *Cluid* stoope low,
The Vale, that bred thee pure, as her Hills Snow.

From thence, display thy wing againe
    Over *Iërna* maine,
    To the *Eugenian* dale;
        There charme the rout
With thy soft notes, and hold them within Pale
        That late were out.
    Musicke hath power to draw,
Where neither Force can bend, nor Feare can awe.

Be proofe, the glory of his hand,
    (*Charles Montjoy*) whose command
    Hath all beene Harmony:
        And more hath wonne
Upon the *Kerne*, and wildest *Irishry*,
        Then Time hath donne,
    Whose strength is above strength;
And conquers all things, yea it selfe, at length.

Who ever sipt at *Baphyre* river,
    That heard but Spight deliver
    His farre-admired Acts,
        And is not rap't
With entheate rage, to publish their bright tracts?
        (But this more apt
    When him alone we sing)
Now must we plie our ayme; our Swan's on wing.

Who (see) already hath ore-flowne
    The *Hebrid* Isles, and knowne

The scatter'd *Orcades*;
    From thence is gon
To utmost *Thule*: whence, he backes the Seas
    To *Caledon*,
   And over *Grampius* mountaine,
To *Loumond* lake, and *Twedes* blacke-springing fountaine.

Haste, Haste, sweete Singer: Nor to *Tine*,
   Humber, or *Owse*, decline;
   But over Land to *Trent*:
    There coole thy Plumes,
And up againe, in skies, and aire to vent
    Their reeking fumes;
   Till thou at *Tames* alight,
From whose prowde bosome, thou began'st thy flight.

Tames, prowde of thee, and of his Fate
   In entertaining late
   The choise of *Europes* pride;
    The nimble *French*;
The *Dutch* whom Wealth (not Hatred) doth divide;
    The *Danes* that drench
   Their cares in wine; with sure
Though slower *Spaine*; and *Italy* mature.

All which, when they but heare a straine
   Of thine, shall thinke the *Maine*
   Hath sent her *Mermaides* in,
    To hold them here:
Yet, looking in thy face, they shall begin
    To loose that feare;
   And (in the place) envie
So blacke a Bird, so bright a Qualitie.

But should they know (as I) that this,
   Who warbleth PANCHARIS,
   Were CYCNUS, once high flying
    With *Cupids* wing;

Though, now by *Love* transform'd, & dayly dying:
    (Which makes him sing
  With more delight, and grace)
Or thought they, *Leda*'s white Adult'rers place

Among the starres should be resign'd
  To him, and he there shrin'd;
  Or *Tames* be rap't from us
    To dimme and drowne
In heav'n the Signe of old *Eridanus*:
    How they would frowne!
  But these are Mysteries
Conceal'd from all but cleare Propheticke eyes.

It is inough, their griefe shall know
  At their returne, nor *Po*,
  Iberus, Tagus, Rheine,
    Scheldt, nor the *Maas,*
Slow *Arar*, nor swift *Rhone*; the *Loyre*, nor *Seine,*
    With all the race
  Of *Europes* waters can
Set out a like, or second to our Swan.

To the memory of my beloved,

The Author Mr William Shakespeare:

And what he hath left us

To draw no envy (*Shakespeare*) on thy name,
  Am I thus ample to thy Booke, and Fame:
While I confesse thy writings to be such,
  As neither *Man*, nor *Muse*, can praise too much.
'Tis true, and all mens suffrage. But these wayes
  Were not the paths I meant unto thy praise:
For seeliest Ignorance on these may light,
  Which, when it sounds at best, but eccho's right;
Or blinde Affection, which doth ne're advance
  The truth, but gropes, and urgeth all by chance;
Or crafty Malice, might pretend this praise,
  And thinke to ruine, where it seem'd to raise.
These are, as some infamous Baud, or Whore,
  Should praise a Matron. What could hurt her more?
But thou art proofe against them, and indeed
  Above th'ill fortune of them, or the need.
I, therefore will begin. Soule of the Age!
  The applause! delight! the wonder of our Stage!
My *Shakespeare*, rise; I will not lodge thee by
  Chaucer, or *Spenser*, or bid *Beaumont* lye
A little further, to make thee a roome:
  Thou art a Moniment, without a tombe,
And art alive still, while thy Booke doth live,
  And we have wits to read, and praise to give.
That I not mixe thee so, my braine excuses;
  I meane with great, but disproportion'd *Muses*:
For, if I thought my judgement were of yeeres,
  I should commit thee surely with thy peeres,
And tell, how farre thou didst our *Lily* out-shine,
  Or sporting *Kid*, or *Marlowes* mighty line.

And though thou hadst small *Latine*, and lesse *Greeke*,
    From thence to honour thee, I would not seeke
For names; but call forth thund'ring *Aeschilus*,
    Euripides, and *Sophocles* to us,
Paccuvius, *Accius*, him of *Cordova* dead,
    To life againe, to heare thy Buskin tread,
And shake a Stage: Or, when thy Sockes were on,
    Leave thee alone, for the comparison
Of all, that insolent *Greece*, or haughtie *Rome*
    Sent forth, or since did from their ashes come.
Triúmph, my *Britaine*, thou hast one to showe,
    To whom all Scenes of *Europe* homage owe.
He was not of an age, but for all time!
    And all the *Muses* still were in their prime,
When like *Apollo* he came forth to warme
    Our eares, or like a *Mercury* to charme!
Nature her selfe was proud of his designes,
    And joy'd to weare the dressing of his lines!
Which were so richly spun, and woven so fit,
    As, since, she will vouchsafe no other Wit.
The merry *Greeke*, tart *Aristophanes*,
    Neat *Terence*, witty *Plautus*, now not please;
But antiquated, and deserted lye
    As they were not of Natures family.
Yet must I not give Nature all: Thy Art,
    My gentle *Shakespeare*, must enjoy a part.
For though the *Poets* matter, Nature be,
    His Art doth give the fashion. And, that he,
Who casts to write a living line, must sweat,
    (Such as thine are) and strike the second heat
Upon the *Muses* anvile: turne the same,
    (And himselfe with it) that he thinkes to frame;
Or for the lawrell, he may gaine a scorne,
    For a good *Poet*'s made, as well as borne.
And such wert thou. Looke how the fathers face
    Lives in his issue, even so, the race

Of *Shakespeares* minde, and manners brightly shines
   In his well torned, and true-filed lines:
In each of which, he seemes to shake a Lance,
   As brandish't at the eyes of Ignorance.
Sweet Swan of *Avon*! what a sight it were
   To see thee in our waters yet appeare,
And make those flights upon the bankes of *Thames*,
   That so did take *Eliza*, and our *James*!
But stay, I see thee in the *Hemisphere*
   Advanc'd, and made a Constellation there!
Shine forth, thou Starre of *Poets*, and with rage,
   Or influence, chide, or cheere the drooping Stage;
Which, since thy flight from hence, hath mourn'd like night,
   And despaires day, but for thy Volumes light.

The just indignation the *Author* tooke at the vulgar
censure of his *Play*, by some malicious spectators,
begat this following *Ode* to himselfe.

Come leave the lothed stage,
  And the more lothsome age:
Where pride, and impudence (in faction knit)
    Usurpe the chaire of wit!
Indicting, and arraigning every day
    Something they call a Play.
  Let their fastidious, vaine
  Commission of the braine
Run on, and rage, sweat, censure, and condemn:
They were not made for thee, lesse, thou for them.

Say, that thou pour'st them wheat,
  And they will acornes eat:
'Twere simple fury, still, thy selfe to waste
    On such as have no taste!
To offer them a surfet of pure bread,
    Whose appetites are dead!
  No, give them graines, their fill,
  Huskes, draffe to drinke, and swill.
If they love lees, and leave the lusty wine,
Envy them not, their palate's with the swine.

No doubt some mouldy tale,
  Like *Pericles*; and stale
As the Shrieves crusts, and nasty as his fish-scraps, out of
            every dish,
Throwne forth, and rak't into the common tub,
    May keepe up the *Play-club*:
  There, sweepings doe as well
  As the best order'd meale.
For, who the relish of these ghests will fit,
Needs set them, but, the almes-basket of wit.

And much good do't you then:
  Brave *plush*, and *velvet*-men;
Can feed on orts: And safe in your stage-clothes,
    Dare quit, upon your oathes,
The stagers, and the stage-wrights too (your peeres)
    Of larding your large eares
  With their foule *comick* socks;
  Wrought upon twenty blocks:
Which, if they are torne, and turn'd, & patch't enough,
The gamesters share your guilt, and you their stuffe.

  Leave things so prostitute,
  And take the *Alcaick* Lute;
Or thine owne *Horace*, or *Anacreons* Lyre;
    Warme thee, by *Pindares* fire:
And though thy nerves be shrunke, and blood be cold,
    Ere yeares have made thee old;
  Strike that disdaine-full heate
  Throughout, to their defeate:
As curious fooles, and envious of thy straine,
May, blushing, sweare no palsey's in thy braine.

  But, when they heare thee sing
  The glories of thy *King*,
His zeale to *God*, and his just awe o're men;
    They may, blood-shaken, then,
Feele such a flesh-quake to possesse their powers:
    As they shall cry, like ours
  In sound of peace, or warres,
  No Harpe ere hit the starres;
In tuning forth the acts of his sweet raigne:
And raysing *Charles* his chariot, 'bove his *Waine*.

To my old Faithfull Servant: and (by his continu'd
Vertue) my loving Friend: the Author of this Work,
M. Rich. Brome

I had you for a Servant, once, *Dick Brome*;
    And you perform'd a Servants faithfull parts:
Now, you are got into a nearer roome,
    Of *Fellowship*, professing my old Arts.
And you doe doe them well, with good applause,
    Which you have justly gained from the *Stage*,
By observation of those Comick Lawes
    Which I, your *Master*, first did teach the Age.
You learn'd it well; and for it, serv'd your time
    A Prentise-ship: which few doe now a dayes.
Now each Court-Hobby-horse will wince in rime;
    Both learned, and unlearned, all write *Playes*.
It was not so of old: Men tooke up trades
    That knew the Crafts they had bin bred in, right:
An honest *Bilbo*-Smith would make good blades,
    And the *Physician* teach men spue, or shite;
        The *Cobler* kept him to his nall; but, now
        Hee'll be a *Pilot*, scarce can guide a Plough.

Ode

If Men, and tymes were nowe
   Of that true Face
As when they both were greate, and both knewe howe
   That Fortune to embrace,
By Cherisshing the Spirrites that gave their greatnesse grace:
   I then could rayse my notes
   Lowd to the wondringe thronge
And better Blason them, then all their Coates,
That were the happie subject of my songe.

Butt, Clownishe pride hath gott
   Soe much the starte
Of Civill virtue, that hee now is not
   Nor cann be of desert,
That hath not Countrye impudence enough to laughe
     att Arte,
   Whilest lyke a blaze of strawe,
   Hee dyes with an ill sent,
To every sence, and scorne to those that sawe
Howe soone with a selfe ticklinge hee was spent.

Breake then thie quills, blott out
   Thie long watch'd verse
And rather to the Fyre, then to the Rowte
   Their labour'd tunes reherse,
Whose ayre will sooner Hell, then their dull senses peirce;
   Thou that doest spend thie dayes
   To gett thee a leane Face,
And come forth worthie Ivye, or the Bayes,
And in this Age, canst hope no other grace.
Yett: since the bright, and wyse,
   Mynerva deignes
Uppon soe humbled earth to cast hir eyes:
   Wee'l rip our Richest veynes

And once more stryke the eare of tyme with those fresh
      straynes:
   As shall besides delyght
   And Cunninge of their grownde
Give cause to some of wonnder, some despite,
But unto more dispayre to imitate their sounde.

Throwe, Holy Virgin, then
   Thie Chrystall shield
Aboute this Isle, and Charme the rounde, as when
   Thou mad'st in open Feild
The Rebell Gyantes stoope, and Gorgon Envye yeild,
   Cause Reverence, if not Feare,
   Throughout their generall breastes,
And by their takinge, lett it once appeare
Whoe worthie winne, whoe not, to bee wyse Pallas guests.

Notes

The old punctuation and spelling may be difficult at first to one who is not used to them, but many apparent obscurities can be cleared up by a careful reading aloud. Thus, for example *cop'ces* and *cullors* appear unfamiliar until the reader realizes that they are *copses* and *colours*.

I list here a few peculiarities of the seventeenth-century text which might cause difficulty, but which occur too often to be noted each time.

to is sometimes printed for *too*

thorough and *through* are often interchangeable spellings; so are *then* and *than*

apostrophes may be used to indicate elision, thus *t'have* or *to' have*, and *w'are* or *we'are* should each be read aloud as one syllable

many possessive apostrophes are omitted, thus *the cannons rage* where we would write *the cannon's* (or *the cannons'*) *rage*

the ending *-ed* is usually pronounced: thus *returned* is three syllables, and *return'd* is two.

In the following notes to the poems I have had a great deal of help from C. H. Herford, Percy and Evelyn Simpson's eleven-volume edition of Jonson's works (O.U.P., 1925–51). Of other editions, the one I found most useful was John Hollander's selection of Jonson's poetry in the Laurel Poetry Series (Dell, 1961).

Echo's Song, page 3 line 4: division – (a) the dividing of slow notes into quick ones; (b) separation (from a person).

Song ('Fooles, they are . . .'), page 5, line 10: free from slaughter – with impunity.

Hymen's Speech, page 8, line 10: priest of peace – i.e. James I, present at the wedding where this masque was performed. The 'Union' referred to is that of England and Scotland under one king.

Charms of the Witches, page 11, line 22: Cat-a-Mountaine – wild cat.

page 12, lines 4 & 5: i.e. they used their nails to dig the ditch where they would bury images.

page 12, line 9: little Martin – 'Theyr little Martin is hee, that calls them to theyr Conventicles: which is done in a humane voyce; but, comming forth, they find him in the shape of a great Buck-Goate, upon whome they ride to theyre meetings' (Jonson's note).

page 12, line 10: merely – merrily.

page 12, line 11: a thorne – bramble (here used as a whip).

Father Christmas' Song: Herford and Simpson say that in the masque
from which this comes Johnson is 'burlesquing a Christmas
performance [of a mummers' play] at a City hall.'

page 16. line 7: Love – Cupid. Father Christmas is introducing
characters as they come on stage.

page 16, line 8: pulls himself into the affair (the masque) too.

page 16, line 11: stake – pole to dance round, like a Maypole.

page 16, line 17: what you lack – the shopkeeper's greeting.

page 17, line 28: keepeth – lives.

Song for Comus: Jonson calls Comus 'the god of cheere, or the belly'.

page 19, lines 5–7: Hoppar – big funnel in a corn-mill; hutch – trough
used by bakers for kneading dough; bowlter – cloth for sifting;
coppar – large copper receptacle; bavin – brushwood used as fuel by
bakers; mawkin – mop for cleaning out a baker's oven; peele –
baker's shovel.

page 19, line 11: hyppocras bag – bag used to strain a mulled wine called
hippocras.

page 19, line 12: swag – Fatty!

page 19, line 19: sod – boiled.

Two Songs sung by Daedalus, page 20, line 7: she – i.e. Pleasure. Pleasure
and Virtue showed the young Hercules two paths to choose between.

page 20, line 13: numerous – rhythmical.

page 21, line 1: ground – source.

Gypsy Song, page 22, line 4: Aegiptians – gypsies.

page 22, line 16: cut your laces – faint.

page 22, line 23: Burly – place where the masque was presented.

page 22, line 24: hurly – commotion.

Two Gypsy Songs, page 23, line 5: firedrake – fiery dragon.

Sea Song, page 24 line 7: Pallas (Athene) and Arachne had a contest in
weaving. When Arachne won it, she was turned into a spider.

page 24, line 17: amber-gris – grey amber.

To my Booke, page 32, line 13: departs – parts.

To William Camden: Camden had been Jonson's school-master, and had
written books about Britain.

On Chev'rill the Lawyer: Chev'rill – kid leather (which is flexible and
easily stretched).

page 38, line 1: leese – lose.

On Margaret Ratcliffe, page 39, line 15: she died of grief for her brother's
death.

On My First Sonne, page 41, line 1: right hand – the meaning of the name
Benjamin in Hebrew.

page 41, line 10: *poetrie* – a poet is both in Greek and in medieval
English a 'maker'.

page 41, line 12: Hugh Maclean comments that this line appears to reflect 'the classical belief that excessive good fortune is likely to excite the jealousy of the gods' and quotes Martial, Epigrams VI, xxix, 8: 'quidquid ames, capias non placuisse nimis', which he translates 'whatever you love, may you wish not to have been overly pleased by it'. *Ben Jonson and the Caroline Poets* (Norton).

To Play-wright, page 42, line 3: salt – wit.

To Lucy Countesse of Bedford, page 48, line 1: brightness – 'Lucy' comes from the Latin *lux* (light).

To John Donne, page 49, line 1: where – whether.

page 49, line 10: pui'nees – juniors.

page 49, line 11: burst – break.

Inviting a friend to supper, page 50, line 16: there was a saying 'When the sky falls, we shall have larks'.

page 50, lines 19–20: godwit, etc. – the names of birds.

page 51, line 3: *Pooly*', or *Parrot* – government spies. Pooly had betrayed Babington and had been present at Marlowe's murder.

Epitaph on Salomon Pavy: he had been a boy actor.

page 53, line 15: *Parcae* – the Fates.

On the Famous Voyage: a parody of mythological journeys through the underworld.

page 56, line 8: our – ours; in one – in the Fleet Ditch.

page 56 line 28: three for one – as insurance on foreign travel.

page 59, line 13: *sough* – sigh; lurden – layabout.

page 59, line 15: *Paris-garden* – where bear baiting took place.

page 59, line 16: KATE ARDEN – a famous whore.

page 59, line 18: foist – (a) state barge; (b) bad smell.

page 59, line 31: nare – nostril.

page 60, line 8: houghs – hocks.

page 60, line 11: flead – flayed.

page 60, line 14: convince – convict.

page 60, line 17: *Tibert* – Tibby.

page 60, line 35: *Plague*-bill – list of those killed by plague.

page 61, line 22: A-JAX – pronounced 'a jakes'.

The Forrest. Jonson explains the title for this part of his works in a prefatory note to *The Underwood*. The poems in *The Forrest* are 'workes of divers nature, and matter congested'. *The Underwood* consists of 'lesser Poems, of later growth'.

To Penshurst, page 66, line 2: touch – fine black marble.

page 66, line 14: his great birth – i.e. Sir Philip Sidney's. Penshurst was the estate of the Sidney family.

page 67, line 3: officiously – dutifully.

page 68, line 5: livorie – provisions.

To Sir Robert Wroth, page 70, line 11: mast – acorns, beechnuts, chestnuts.
   page 70, line 28: leese – lose.
   page 71, line 6: jarre – clash.
To the World, page 73, line 24: gyves – fetters.
   page 74, line 2: engines – contrivances.
   page 74, line 24: grutch – complain.
'*Not to know vice at all*', page 79, line 15: taste – test.
   page 79, line 16: close – secret.
   page 81, line 1: Luxurie – lust.
   page 81, line 33: feature – form.
   page 82, line 12: securely – carelessly, confidently.
Ode. To Sir William Sidney, page 84, line 9: nephew – i.e. Sir Philip's.
   page 84 line 26: bone-fires – bonfires.
To Heaven, page 85, line 2: bee – i.e. seem.
A Celebration of Charis, page 91, line 6: scope – aim.
   page 91, line 16: wreake – revenge.
   page 92, line 16: nard – an aromatic herb.
   page 93, line 21: proyne – preen.
   page 93, line 23: i.e. in the Iliad.
   page 93, line 32: the Apple – refers to the Judgment of Paris, who had to
      award the golden apple to whichever was the fairest among Juno,
      Minerva and Venus.
   page 96, line 17: say over every purle – try over every knitted loop (purl
      as in the stitch in knitting).
   page 96, line 19: Secretarie – maid.
   page 96, line 20: *Fucus* – paint or dye.
   page 97, line 30: stake – pole, post.
   page 97, line 31: Brake – 'a frame for vicious colts while they were shod'
      (Herford and Simpson).
In the person of Woman-kind, page 100, line 11: parcels – bits.
   page 100, line 14: curious peece – skilful work.
My Picture left in Scotland, page 103, line 7: close – cadence.
An Epitaph on Master Vincent Corbet, page 106, line 4: Corbet's son wrote
   an elegy on him; it is not known who the friend was.
   page 106, line 16: Nourceries – nurseries (he was a gardener).
   page 106, line 21: specious – splendid.
An Elegie ('Though Beautie be'), page 108, line 5: Allay – alloy.
   page 108, line 25: Dietie – deity.
An Ode. To himselfe, page 110, line 4: Securitie – complacency.
   page 110, line 9: Clarius – Apollo.
   page 1110, line 11: Pies – magpies.
   page 110, line 27: *Japhets* lyne – Prometheus; aspire – inspire.
   page 110, line 30: the issue of *Joves* braine – Minerva.

A Fit of Rime against Rime, page 113, line 15: *ceasure* – caesura.

An Epitaph, page 114, line 4: Upon – on.

An Elegie (' 'Tis true, I'm broke'), page 115, line 18: defeat – undo.
    page 117, line 30: Chore – company.

An Elegie ('That Love's a bitter sweet'), page 119, line 23: Dark-lanterne – a
covered lantern.

An Elegie ('Let me be what I am'), page 123, line 9: the slang sense of
'occupy' was 'make love'.
    page 124, line 2: Spittle Sermon – refers to an annual sermon preached
    near the site of the old Hospital ('Spittle') of St Mary's.

An Execration upon Vulcan: occasioned by a fire which destroyed Jonson's
MSS. in 1623.
    page 125, line 8: clos'd in horne – lanterns had translucent horn where
    later glass was used.
    page 125, line 10: a horn lantern, thus a cuckold's horns.
    page 125, lines 29–30: – i.e. romances.
    page 126, lines 2–7: – i.e. poems in which, Jonson implies, the elaborate
    form is of more importance than the content. Some poems were
    written so that their shapes on the page resembled the shapes of
    their subjects (George Herbert wrote several, 'The Altar', 'Easter
    Wings', etc.).
    page 126, line 7: jumpe – exactly corresponding.
    page 127, line 10: strong lines – what we nowadays call Metaphysical
    poetry.
    page 127, line 17: accite – excite.
    page 127, lines 21–2: 'A translation of the *Ars Poetica* of Horace
    illustrated from the *Poetics* of Aristotle. The scholarship of Jonson's
    day held that Horace was "taught" by Aristotle' (Herford and
    Simpson). *Venusine* – presumably Horace is called this because
    he also wrote the *Art of Love; Stagirite* – Aristotle was born in
    Stageira.
    page 128, line 16: a *Vulcanale* – a hymn to Vulcan.
    page 128, line 25: meere – complete.
    page 128, line 31: Chambers – cannons fired during the performance of
    Shakespeare's *Henry VIII* which started the fire that burned down the
    Globe Theatre.
    page 128, line 36: Stewes – brothels.
    page 129, line 2: *Winchestrian* Goose – syphilis.
    page 129, line 6: the beares – i.e. in the nearby Bear Garden.
    page 129, line 8: *Kate Arden* – a whore (or nun of Venus).
    page 129, line 13: *Fortune* – The Fortune Theatre, which had also
    burned down; as had the Banqueting House at Whitehall (line 24),
    the Six Clerk's Office in Chancery Lane (page 155, line 6), the

Glasse-house, a glass factory (line 14), and, in 1561, the steeple of Old Saint Paul's (line 27).

page 130, line 4: fats – vats.

page 130, line 11: *Bell*-Man – night watchman.

page 130, line 22: Glaves – broadswords.

page 130, line 23: *Bilbo* – Bilboa, where the best blades were made.

page 130, line 25: The Fryar – Roger Bacon.

page 130, line 30: Granats – grenades.

page 131, line 4: *Bess Broughton* – a famous whore.

An Epistle answering to one . . .: 'The scriptural phrase "sealed in the tribe of Benjamin" . . . is adapted to Ben's "sons" who gathered around him in the Apollo' (Herford and Simpson).

page 132, line 32: *Val-telline* – a strategic valley in the Grisons.

page 133, line 1: States – the Dutch.

page 133, line 3: Dispensation – for Prince Charles to marry the Infanta of Spain.

page 133 line 12: *Brunsfield* and *Mansfield* – soldiers.

page 133, line 16: Inigo Jones was one of the people put in charge of the entertainment for the Infanta at Southampton in 1623. Jonson sees Jones, his rival at Court, as superseding him. 'His', in the next line, refers to Jones.

page 133, line 17: not under-heares – is not reported inferior.

page 133, line 32: wel-tagde – well-fastened, well-knit.

page 133, line 34: Scenes – as created by Inigo Jones, for example.

To the immortall memorie . . .: Sir Henry Morison had died in 1629. This poem is the first Pindaric Ode attempted in English. The turne, counter-turne, and stand correspond to the strophe, antistrophe, and epode in Greek.

page 135, line 1: cleare – it may be useful to remember that the Latin *clarus* meant famous.

page 135, line 9: a circle and page 162 line 2: the Spheare – i.e. the perfect form. 'The perfect'st figure is the round,' says Reason in *Hymenaei*.

page 138, line 5: *Asterisme* – constellation.

page 138, line 9: *Dioscuri* – Gemini.

page 139, line 13: rowles – rolls, archives.

An Elegie on Lady Jane Pawlet, page 141, line 2: Yewgh – yew.

page 141, line 10: i.e. Thomas, Viscount Savage, of Rock Savage in Cheshire.

page 141, line 25: dotes – gifts.

page 141, line 27: Carract – carat, value.

page 142 line 2: inlive – animate.

Eupheme: the title is coined by Jonson from the Greek, 'of good omen' or

'Faire Fame'. The epigraph at the beginning is translated by John
Hollander: 'To love her in life is a pleasure, in death a pious devotion.'
Hollander translates the epigraph to part 9, 'Late, indeed, is the balm
prepared for so great a sorrow,' and the epigraph at the end of the
whole poem, 'In memory of your Venetia's piety, to which you, her
worthy husband, attest, I dedicate this apotheosis, O Digby, to you
and yours.'

page 145 line 6: CREPUNDIA – a child's rattle, i.e. childish toys.

page 145, line 13: prime Coates – a child's first short clothes.

page 145, line 18: Call's – cauls.

page 145, line 23: take tent – take heed.

page 145 line 28: 'gree – degree.

page 146 line 1: uncontrol'd – undisputed.

page 151, line 2: sey'd – assayed.

page 151, line 18: cleies – claws.

page 152, line 12: 'greet – weep for or regret.

page 153, line 6: interpell – break in upon.

page 153, line 21: – and there now follow the hierarchies of
Heaven.

page 155, line 29: gate – pace.

Ode. Allegorike: printed in Hugh Holland's *Pancharis* (1603). Holland is
the black swan.

page 161, line 8: *Tamisis* – Thames (later in the poem spelled
Tames).

page 162, line 6: *Mône* – Anglesey.

page 162, line 7: *Cluid* – Clwyn in Denbighshire, where Holland came
from.

page 162, line 10: *Iërna* maine – the Irish Sea.

page 162, line 21: *Kerne* – Irish foot soldier.

page 162, line 29: entheate – inspired; tracts – tracks, career.

page 163, line 24: the *Maine* – the sea.

page 164, line 9: *Eridanus* – the Po, which ended up as a
constellation.

To the memory of my beloved . . .: originally printed at the beginning of
the First Folio of Shakespeare's Works (1623).

page 165, line 7: seeliest – simplest.

page 166, line 5: him of *Cordova* dead – Seneca.

page 166, line 7: Sockes – light shoes worn by actors in ancient Greek
and Roman comedy.

Ode to himself: occasioned by the failure of his play *The New Inne*, and
originally printed at the end of it.

page 168, line 18: draffe – hog's wash.

page 168, line 24: the common tub – 'the refuse of the table at City feasts and at Court was collected by the servants . . . and put into a large basket for the poor' (Herford and Simpson).

page 169, line 3: orts – scraps.

page 169, line 8: blocks – molds.

page 169, line 30: The Great Bear is still sometimes called Charles' Wain (or wagon). Originally the Charles was Charlemagne; here Jonson refers to Charles I.

To my old faithfull servant . . . page 170, line 15: *Bilbo*-smith – sword-smith.

page 170, line 17: nall – awl.